THE BILLIONAIRE WITHIN

How to Develop a Positive Money Philosophy
and
Maximize Six Black Box Secrets to Wealth Mastery

KENNETH PORTER

LEGAL DISCLAIMER & DISCLOSURE

CONTENTS

ACKNOWLEDGEMENTS

The work of an author cannot be considered solely the expression of his or her ideas. The concepts and money philosophies that have formed in my mind are the result of interactions both good and bad with people I have crossed paths with over the last twenty plus years of my career.

I wish to express my gratitude for the wonderful people who helped and encouraged me to write *The Billionaire Within.*

First and foremost, I would like to thank my Lord and Savior, Jesus Christ, for giving me His gift of eternal life. I would also like to thank Him for showing such favor in my life. Even through the valleys, trials and tribulations, He has been faithful to me. Thank you, Lord.

To my wife Kathleen, you are my rock and greatest support. Thank you for your countless sacrifices. Only you will ever know the true joy and pain we both have shared over the years. Without your unwavering love, support and encouragement, I would never have made it this far in life; much less finished this book. May God bless us with a billion more precious memories and meaningful experiences to share in life. I love you dearly sweetheart.

To my five children and daughter-in-law, thank you for your encouragement and understanding. You are the best kids a father could ever ask for. I pray that God richly blesses all of your lives. I believe God has great things on the horizon for all of you. Trust Him and continue to believe that with hard work, dedication and commitment your dreams will come true. Failures may come, but never, ever give up on your dreams and goals. I love you, Noah, Sarah, Jacob, Isaiah, Elizabeth and Sarah, my lovely daughter-in-law.

I am also grateful for Kathleen's parents and their love, support and unwavering commitment to family. Mark and Paula, you guys are awesome. Thank you from the bottom of my heart. A big 2!

Thank you to my support team, who helped me accomplish this personal goal. I am especially grateful for my editor Lydia Wheeler and my creative web developer Mark Heinsman. This would have been virtually impossible without you guys. Thank you.

Unfortunately, my parents did not live long enough to this goal achieved, but I know they are smiling down on me. Thank you Mom and Dad for all the good you poured into my life. I love you both and think of you often.

To my sister Kathy and her husband Ken, thank you for being there for us when we needed it most. Kathy, get to work on that book and Ken, believe in the possibilities.

Lastly, I would like to thank my many mentors, instructors, teachers and coaches who trained me either personally or through online courses. Thank you, Jack Canfield, Brendon Burchard, the late David H. Sandler and all the other coaches and trainers who help thousands of entrepreneurs find their best self each and every day. Thanks to Ronald Dukes for giving me my start in the financial business. Thank you Ed Stein, Bob Castiglione, Stan Kacala, Bob Ball, Don Blanton and all the other financial experts and trainers who had a huge impact on my financial awareness, knowledge and career. I would also like to thank my clients who entrusted me to play a part in their wealth-purposed plans. May God bless you as you continue to develop a positive money philosophy and find *The Billionaire Within*™.

FOREWORD

For many of us, the topics of financial planning and wealth management can seem overwhelming. Often we are bombarded with TV shows, radio shows, commercials and advertisements all directed at telling us how to save for retirement, how to get rich quick, what to buy, what not to buy, what *not* to do with your money, what *to* do with your money; sometimes the same advice is used to support opposite views at the same time! It is enough to make you throw your hands up in and say, "Forget it! I'll sleep with my money under my mattress!" Or worse, you give up control and walk into someone's office and say, "Here, take my money and tell me what to do with it." That's where I was nine months ago before I met Kenny. I was 37, divorced, had a stable job, owned a house, had been dutiful in socking away money in my employer sponsored retirement plan, and scared to death that I had no cash flow, no liquid savings to speak of, no long- term savings plan and no wealth building goals of any sort.

I found myself staring into a dark tunnel leading toward my future and I had no idea what was on the other side. Sometimes timing is everything and at the moment I was staring into the darkness, a friend suggested I talk to Kenny. I was nervous and embarrassed that I was so far behind in planning my financial future.

It's funny, I measure our nation's economy for a living, I immerse myself in economic statistics and financial data on a daily basis, but when it came to my own personal economic well-being, I was a passive spectator. I wasn't an active participant in shaping my own economic future. I knew I couldn't put this off any longer. I needed to take control. I just didn't know how to start. By the time I finished my first conversation with Kenny, he was already shining a light into the darkness.

Kenny quickly earned my trust because at the core of his philosophy on money and wealth were the principles of hard work, personal responsibility, and accountability for one's actions, all principles by which I live my own life. I doubt that all the Google searching in the world would have found a better matched advisor than Kenny. At the core of Kenny's message is his belief that personal responsibility and accountability combined with basic, common sense economic principles form the cornerstone for building long-term financial happiness. His experiences both good and bad as a financial advisor, entrepreneur, investor and businessman make him uniquely qualified to help us navigate through financial industry rhetoric and the myths, to focus on what matters: how money, the economy and the financial markets work, and more importantly, how to make them work for us.

Kenny Porter wrote *The Billionaire Within* because he wants to help as many people as he can take control of their own economic happiness. This book outlines the same principles that he shares with his individual clients and that he practices himself.

For those of you looking for a financial panacea or a wonder pill that will solve all your financial ills, you won't find it in this book. What you will find is a set of guiding principles designed to help each of us discover our individual philosophy on money, develop the knowledge and confidence to make informed economic decisions anchored to that philosophy, and achieve the goals we set for ourselves.

I am indebted to Kenny for the council and guidance he provided me. I am so very happy he is able to share his knowledge and ideas with so many people through this book.

Thank you, Kenny.
Nicole Mayerhauser

Nicole Mayerhauser is a Division Chief at the National Income and Wealth Division at the Bureau of Economic Analysis, United States Department of Commerce.

INTRODUCTION

Have you ever made a financial decision and regretted it? Do you find yourself making financial decisions based solely on the opinions of friends, coworkers, media and well-meaning family members? Have you been putting off a major financial decision because you're paralyzed by information overload? Does the constant bombardment of financial marketing have you in a proverbial tailspin? Have you really considered what you financially believe to be true and why?

The Billionaire Within™ will guide you in how to develop your own positive money philosophy so you can maneuver through your financial life with confidence by discovering:

- How to harness the wealth eroding effects of procrastination.
- How to cope and manage past financial decisions that ended poorly.
- What's not working financially and how to admit it.
- How to shape and develop new money behaviors.
- Your personal wealth purpose.
- How to decide, commit and execute your money purpose.

The Billionaire Within™ will then transition to show you how to maximize the six black box secrets of wealth mastery. The book will focus on six common financial misconceptions and pitfalls that plague the middle class. The book will challenge you to examine not only your money philosophy, but also the financial decisions that are a direct result of a past money belief. You will be guided on a journey to examine what you believe to be true regarding:

- The future of taxation in our country.
- The real current benefit and future value of your 401(k).
- Why you own real estate.
- The "magic" of compound interest in taxable accounts.
- How to fund your child's college education.
- Death insurance and life insurance.
- Mastering a wealth-purposed plan.

You may find that much of what is being said in *The Billionaire Within*™ might seem counterintuitive. You may also feel yourself getting angry that your current financial advisors have not sounded the alarm for you regarding the information I expose. If you do find that the information seems contrary to your current belief system, ask yourself, *"What if?"*

What if the information I have shared with you turns out to be true? Financial events will occur in life, some good and some bad. Your financial outcome depends overwhelmingly on how you respond to them. This book is my effort to get the elusive financial truths out of the "black box" and specifically into the hands of the middle class.

1

The Auction Paddle Effect

To get through the hardest journey we need take only
one step at a time, but we must keep on stepping.
- Ancient Chinese Proverb

Over 33 years ago, when I was a 10-year-old boy, I experienced my first taste of business and commerce. My Uncle Robert owned a small 23-acre farm in Orange County, N.C. At any given time he had about twenty head of Black Angus cattle. On occasion he would take me with him to the auction. He not only bought and sold cattle for profit, he slaughtered a few each year for himself and close family to consume. It made him quite popular in our family circle.

One summer morning he allowed me to tag along and we discussed the auction scheme of the day. He was interested in buying some young heifers to breed with Hercules, the local Black Angus stud. By doing so, he could increase the herd without having to go to the auction house and purchase more cattle. Little did I know this would be my first lesson in money principles, or what I call having a positive money philosophy. We will discuss that topic later in this book and in detail at our exclusive member community - **The Black Box Society™.**

Uncle Robert explained to me that once he had enough heifers he could increase his own herd without having to purchase cattle from the auction. By breeding cattle he could be on the buy and sell side of the transaction. But we both got more than we bargained for that day. I learned a lesson in life and business I will never forget. It has been more than thirty years, but every time I see a cow I remember that day and chuckle nervously under my breath.

When you enter the cattle auction house they require you sign in and pick a paddle. The number inscribed on it is how the auctioneer identifies you in the bidding process. But as I recall, my uncle ended up in a conversation with one of his old farmer buddies after we got our paddle and had somewhere in the process given it to me to hold for safekeeping. Uncle Robert was not known for being an in-depth conversationalist, but for whatever reason he had become rather long winded on this particular day and I had become rather impatient waiting.

Like most curious boys at that age, I wanted to go in and watch the action unfold. I tugged on my uncle's shirt sleeve and motioned to let him know I was headed into the arena to watch the fun and excitement of cattle commerce in action. If you have ever been to a live cattle auction, or any type of auction for that matter, you can certainly understand the awe and excitement a 10-year-old boy would have in such a venue. The only problem with this entire experience was the unbridled power I held in my right hand. Paddle number 27. For the auctioneer, that paddle represented ultimate discretion, authority and responsibility in the cattle bidding process. For a 10-year-old boy, it represented fun, exhilaration and excitement. I, the safe keeper of paddle number 27, was being acknowledged by the auctioneer and I had just successfully purchased the last three head of steer without any understanding of the unintended consequences. You see, I was given the same power Uncle Robert had by simply possessing paddle number 27, but none of the financial responsibility that came with being the true account holder of paddle number 27.

The unintended consequences of having little knowledge and know-how, and more importantly the financial responsibility my uncle possessed, led to him buying three heifers sight unseen. For me it was exhilarating to bid on that cattle, but costly for my uncle. He unknowingly gave his authority to a 10-year-old, but was still responsible for the actions of that 10-year-old. Needless to say, I do not remember ever attending another auction with my uncle. I did, however, take away a powerful economic lesson from that experience. Unfortunately, the lesson came at an embarrassing and costly price 30 years later.

The silver lining in any tragedy is the choice you have in how you respond. Uncle Robert could not have controlled the event. I had purchased the cattle with the authority of paddle number 27 and he was fully responsible for my actions. The outcome was set in stone. He now owned three new head of cattle. But Uncle

Robert took full responsibility and managed the one and only thing he could control – his response to the event. He made the best of those three head of cattle and bred them for a number of years; hence getting a multiplier effect on the investment I made.

I taught personal financial economics for the first 15 years of my professional life until I sold my wealth planning firm in 2009. My client base included entertainers, musicians, military personnel, executives of large public and private corporations, and hardworking middle-class folks from all walks of life. I was really fortunate and I am thankful to God for having the opportunity to work with some really wonderfully diverse clients from both an asset and community point of view. Having such a diverse sampling of clients gave me a unique insight and understanding. I found that money philosophies and belief systems can have as much or more to do with an individual's outcome than their choice in a financial product. Unfortunately, while I was tending to the financial needs of others in a codependent manor, I was slowly and unintentionally abandoning my own positive money philosophy. Without realizing or acknowledging it, I quickly burned myself out by purchasing a private packaging/fulfillment company in 2008 while simultaneously trying to manage and grow a financial planning firm. I was burning the candle at both ends. By the time I came up for air and assessed where I was personally, professionally and spiritually, I was a paycheck or two away from financial disaster. I later found out my business partner was in deep financial trouble too and facing the devastating effects of a divorce.

I was in the deepest financial, emotional and spiritual debt I had ever experienced. On the outside things seemed great. One friend so eloquently said, "Kenny you must have been born with a golden horseshoe up your rear."

Everything I touched financially seemed to just work in my favor. As a business owner and entrepreneur, I was comfortable with high risk and high reward, but in reality I was experiencing what Alan Greenspan referred to as irrational exuberance.

You see, I had started living a lifestyle with a money philosophy that was flawed and clouded by unbridled influences from my past instead of a money philosophy grounded by the sound principles I learned and taught others early in my career.

My life was similar to that 10-year-old boy with paddle number 27. As housing prices plummeted, financial markets corrected and money flow contracted, I began to feel the devastating financial effects of the economy in my own personal financial macroeconomic world. In four short years, I sold the very successful financial planning business I had grown from scratch while simultaneously acquiring a new packaging company. The business had just over a million in sales when I purchased it and had grown to over $5 million in sales annually.

Then, in what seemed to be a blink of an eye, I was faced with having to restructure a $2.2 million corporate loan and reduce the payment terms from 10 to 5 years. Meanwhile, I was forced to foreclose on two investment properties that were worth over $1.2 million and selling for less than $600,000 each. When my largest client told me they were reducing my contract by 75 percent, it seemed like my company's death knell had been struck. By November 2011, I was hopelessly negotiating with my multi-billion dollar power-tool manufacturing client to come up with alternative contract reduction solutions. I was fending off packaging suppliers to reduce hyper inflated prices and trying to convince my banker that my company could survive this storm. In short, my pleas fell on deaf ears. I was forced into receivership by the bank and had to resign as CEO from my own company. The bank appointed its own manager to dissolve the business and recoup as much of their loan as possible. I was crushed emotionally. I had lost much of my credibility not only from a financial point of view, but professionally and spiritually. I was now unemployed for the first time in my professional career and staring down the barrel of financial ruin. My job over the next few months was to deal with all the personal fallout that would follow on many levels.

I had to back out of purchasing a new home and lost hundreds of thousands in payments and deposits. After hemorrhaging virtually all of our savings, we had to sell many of our personal items to make ends meet. I also had to contact social services to help pay for health care and groceries for our children. Worst of all, I found that people who were friends when times were good, were nowhere to be found when things began to crumble. I was devastated and the world I once knew had come to an abrupt end. My adopted money philosophy had failed me. I was actually starting to experience my very own version of what I have termed *PFTSD,* post financial traumatic stress disorder.

After feeling sorry for myself and licking my wounds for a few months, I realized it was time for a change. At the risk of sounding overly spiritual, the change that was going to occur had to start with my relationship with God. He had forgiven my shortcomings and failures, but I had to deal with my own limited beliefs and head trash. I am so blessed and fortunate to have a loving wife and amazing children. They stayed by my side during my crazy period. After getting some much needed help and support from those who truly loved and cared for me, as well as my family's well-being, I began my road to financial recovery and redemption.

Part of this recovery process was to face the sometimes uncomfortable reality of having to take full responsibility for your own actions. I will discuss this later in the book when I share with you the core principles of a positive money philosophies that helped me stay focused on my journey to financial recovery and find my own billionaire within. As you will discover, *The Billionaire Within* has more to do with your self-worth than the balance of your checkbook.

However, in the second half of this book I will cover six financial decisions that are crucial to the success and survival of the middle class. My goal is to help you discover and understand more clearly the cause and effects of your money decisions as they relate to certain financial products. I will suggest how you can manipulate these products to best fit your own personal macroeconomic plan.

I did not share my experiences for you to pity me or my family. Unfortunately, my story is not that unique. I could write another book, with as many pages as *War and Peace,* telling the stories of people who have gone through much worse than what my family and I experienced. Literally, tens of millions of consumers and businesses have experienced a catastrophic financial event since the 2007 housing and stock market crisis. I hope to use my experiences as a platform in helping others see a better outcome in their own financial life. My second goal is to sound the alarm. While some may not see them, others are ignoring the financial icebergs that face us all in years to come. Remember, it was not what Capt. Edward Smith, of Titanic, saw floating above the water that sank his unsinkable ship.

My overarching desire in writing this book is that you will open your mind to the possibilities of wealth mastery and the relative prosperity that very few achieve, but all desire. I want to be perfectly clear; NO ONE HAS A SILVER BULLET FOR SUCCESS. IT WILL TAKE HARD WORK AND COMMITMENT FROM YOU. True wealth mastery is not a get-rich-quick scheme taught by financial gurus in books, seminars or online today. However, I do believe success gravitates to those who purposely seek it out.

I believe wealth mastery is a laser-focused, systematic execution of sound money philosophies that have been decided upon and committed to over time. There is no single financial product solution for instant wealth. Though financial instruments like paper assets, real estate and enterprise are necessary to achieve wealth, mastery is in knowing how to implement your own money philosophy and personal macroeconomic process.

To become a master of anything, you must acquire knowledge and then become proficient in executing the knowledge you attained. In the spirit of full disclosure: It also means you will have periods of trial and error along the way; maybe even catastrophic failure. If you apply the proven money principles and new financial knowledge attained by reading this book, I believe the following will occur: You will be armed with new knowledge in developing your own positive money philosophy; you will discover the *not-so-secret* secrets to creating the wealth mastery mindset billionaires (inflation adjusted for you economist types) all over the world have known and applied for centuries; and you will be able to verify the existence of limited financial beliefs in your life and the eroding financial factors in your current plan that need to be addressed to find your own billionaire within.

Marilyn vos Savant, Guinness World Record holder for highest *IQ* said, "I believe that much of knowledge is indeed merely memory and this is why so many misconceptions persist for such a long time in the human population. For example, science is rife with error. Because so many people are so thoroughly schooled in the common misconceptions, however, only the most brilliantly skeptical of them will ever discover a mistake. And even then, it will likely be denied for generations to come."

After reading this book you will have a number of decisions to consider as it relates to your personal financial development.

Decisions, however, are void without commitment. But commitment without execution will lead to inevitable failure and the inability to reach your greatest wealth potential. In the spirit of helping you discover and maximize your financial needs and wants, I have created a cloud-based members-only community complete with financial lessons that cover over 20 subjects including how to protect your wealth, save efficiently and potentially grow your assets. We will also have exclusive **Black Box** interviews with experts from various business disciplines dedicated to sharing and helping you discover your own billionaire within. The platform will also have a section for emerging entrepreneurs and seasoned business owners where they can share information, trade business strategies, ask questions and seek professional advice from our vetted business and financial experts. If you want to know more, you can experience the secrets of **The Black Box Society**™ risk-free for 30 days. The society will be growing and changing as we add new content, so stay tuned and stay connected.

I hope you enjoy the book and the words within empower you to *Decide, Commit... & Execute!* ™ your own journey to find a positive money philosophy and the billionaire within.

"Like success, failure is many things to many people. With Positive Mental Attitude, failure is a learning experience, a rung on the ladder, a plateau at which to get your thoughts in order and prepare to try again." - W. Clement Stone

2

What Is a Positive Money Philosophy?

Pos-i-tive Mon-ey Phi-los-o-phy: the rational investigation of money truths and money principles; a set of money views and theories one uses or considers when designing a wealth-purposed plan.

Money impacts how we manage and conduct our daily lives. It creates significant problems when we do not have it, and oddly enough, even more problems when have access to more of it. Money has the unique ability to make us both a master and slave to its control. Some theologians say the Bible makes over 800 references to money and its power over us, second only to the subject of sin. When you add the thoughts of philosophers, economists, statesmen, writers and bloggers all over the world, it is one of the most discussed subjects on the planet. As a matter of fact, while writing this book I decided out of pure curiosity to see how many listings came up when I Googled *money*. The answer – over 2.5 billion results in less than 25 seconds. I think you would agree that while it is one of the most discussed subjects, it is also one of the most misunderstood commodities known to man. Reading this book will solve some of your money mysteries and you will be better equipped to face your financial future with a renewed confidence.

Money is capable of creating partners and rivals, bringing freedom or dependency, and influencing the fate of nations. It is studied in academia as economic science. Modern economic theory focuses on treating money as a means of exchange designed to facilitate trade. Economists study and explain how much money an economy needs and the factors that influence supply and demand.

Analysis of money flow and the global market is certainly important, however, this chapter will focus on the philosophical approach you should adopt. When you are faced with financial challenges and opportunities, you have to have a framework in order to make a confident decision. You then have to have the intestinal fortitude to commit to that decision when it may seem counterintuitive to do so.

Your money beliefs will have a direct effect on your money behaviors. Money behaviors in turn will affect your money relationships and ultimately your money results. When we experience poor financial results, our philosophies are challenged and we tend to make irrational decisions. Consider the events leading to the 2008 stock market crash. The Dow Jones Industrial Average hit its all-time high on October 9, 2007, closing at 14,164.43. Less than two years later, the market had fallen more than 50 percent to 6,594.44, according to CNN Money reports. This, fortunately for all of us alive today, was not the largest decline in history. The market fell by more than 90 percent in a three-year span during the Great Depression. Just like the first crash, there were numerous early warning signs for market correction. The overheated stock and housing market came as early as 2006. Most people, including myself, continued to ignore the warnings and irrationally invested in equities and real estate without an exit strategy or money philosophy.

Think back to this time as it relates to your own personal wealth planning. Did you have a money philosophy in place that addressed how to handle this drastic sell-off, or was the strategy simply to close your eyes, ignore the financial statements and say to yourself, "I'm in this for the long-term?" You should be asking yourself right about now, "What is my own definition of long-term?" And, "what are my entry and exit plans?'" If you are asking yourself these types of questions, you are already developing your money philosophy. The problem, as I stated earlier, is that most people possess an adopted money philosophy, which commonly causes an emotionally charged and reactive behavior that ends in financial disappointment. I suggest developing a money philosophy that becomes proactive by choice, so you can predict a plausible outcome. I am not suggesting that you can predict rates of return, but I am suggesting that your behavior or response has more to do with rates of return than market expansion or contraction. Fundamentally speaking from a macroeconomic view, markets go up in value when there are more buyers than sellers and conversely, markets go down in value when there are more sellers than buyers. When looking at this from your own personal financial macro/microeconomic view, remember that your money philosophy will dictate how you deal with the financial event. Manage the behavior and response to financial events to improve your rate of return. If you are truly committed to changing your financial outcome, you must be prepared to manage your beliefs, behaviors and relationships with money to improve your results.

Please allow me to be very clear and state what should be obvious: rates of return **cannot** be guaranteed by anyone or any institution, nor can financial events be precisely predicted. On the rare occasion that a financial institution makes a guarantee, remember that guarantees for products or services are strictly based on the financial strength and ability of that institution to pay its claim. This is also true for our own federal, state and municipal governments. The only thing you can really control or guarantee is your response to a financial event. How you respond is the key ingredient to having a direct and absolute effect on your bottom line.

The vast majority of financial information in this book is dedicated to educating you on what, I believe, are the six most commonly misunderstood financial instruments and how the limited knowledge in executing these instruments actually erodes the wealth of the ever-shrinking American middle class.

For the middle class to thrive again, I will identify seven core money principles and six financial instruments that must be closely examined in your wealth plan to maximize your return on investment. I believe this statement to be true because I have experienced two common themes with clients all across America while dealing with the understanding of personal finance. The first was a systematic misunderstanding of how money works within a personal money philosophy. Second, I experienced six common financial misconceptions with most middle- to upper-middle-class consumers. It became apparent that most consumers go through life doing what others have done with little to no regard for what is right for their own personal wealth plan. Only you can truly tell what is financially right for you. Therefore, you have to decide for yourself and your family, and take full responsibility for the execution of your money philosophy. Before we dive into the six financial products/instruments, I would like to encourage you to consider and commit to building a positive money philosophy. I have outlined for you what I believe are the seven core principles to developing a positive money philosophy. You may find, while reading my book and developing your money philosophy, that you have other guiding principles through which your money beliefs have been formed. The question you should ask yourself is, "Have I truly decided, committed and executed my core money philosophies?"

SEVEN CORE PRINCIPLES TO DEVELOPING A POSITVE MONEY PHILOSOPHY

1. Learn to Devour Procrastination, One Bite at a Time

Judging from my own personal experiences and working with hundreds of clients over the last fifteen plus years, procrastination exists primarily because of fear of the unknown or taking on too many tasks at one time. Procrastination has been defined as the practice of carrying out more pleasurable tasks over less pleasurable tasks, thus putting off the less pleasurable tasks. We all avoid negative emotions and delay stressful tasks. In some sense we have been brainwashed by society to think we actually work best under pressure, but psychologist Dr. Timothy Pychyl concluded that this belief creates an additional incentive to postpone tasks. Sigmund Freud also called this phenomenon the pleasure principle. Freud said humans instinctually seek pleasure and avoid pain in order to satisfy biological and psychological needs. We all want immediate gratification. In all transparency, I experienced the ill effects of procrastination while writing this book. It was on more occasions than I would like to admit, but it was much easier and more immediately rewarding to stop writing and watch football or go out to lunch with my wife and kids, anything to avoid the task of writing. Those of you who have written or attempted to write a book, thesis or dissertation can easily relate to my battle with procrastination.

If you keep on doing what you have always done with money, then you will keep getting the money results you have always gotten.

Procrastination has killed many well-intended financial goals. How can we break the curse of procrastination? What one, small seemingly insignificant change in your habits could you commit to today to begin squashing the wealth erosion of procrastination? It could be a simple savings commitment that could make all the difference in developing a positive money philosophy. What would seem so trivial today could actually be worth tens of thousands of dollars later in your life without significant change to your lifestyle. Since no one has found the cure-all for procrastination, you will likely read and hear many different prescriptions for what works. Decide what works for you and commit to it. I have compiled a list of techniques to shrink the procrastination monster:

- Just do it! Start with one simple financial goal.
- "Chunk." Break your large financial goals into smaller goals that can be more quickly achieved.
- Find an accountability partner and share your financial desires with them. Ask them to help hold you accountable for your predetermined financial goals.
- Find your "Why?" Knowing your financial "Why?" will help you clarify your "How?"
- *FOCUS* – follow one course until successful. Master one task at a time and accomplish many goals over time!

- List your top six tasks for each day and finish them one at a time until complete. Do not add more tasks until you have completed your initial top six tasks.
- Commit 20 minutes each day to financially educating yourself using our tools in **The Black Box Society**™.
- Reward and celebrate your financial accomplishments.

"A year from now you may wish you had started today."
- Karen Lamb

2. Assume Full Responsibility and Take Control of Your Own Money Decisions

The likelihood of your financial success will diminish as long as you find reasons to blame others for your financial failures. Failures will occur; it is a fact of life in an imperfect world. How you respond to money failure when it occurs will be the deciding factor in how you recover and, more importantly, how quickly you recover. As I mentioned in the introduction, I experienced some devastating financial losses in my business that set in motion a series of significant and catastrophic financial failures. Those failures began to affect my belief system and shortly thereafter my behavior. It wasn't long before those behaviors soured relationships and broke friendships. In the early months of my temporary financial defeat, I looked outwardly for people to blame and hold responsible for what happened. It took hours of prayer, meditation and soul-searching combined with wise coaching to shake my poor behavior and give up all the excuses. Assuming 100 percent responsibility for my actions was and is painful to this day. When I truly surrendered and took full responsibility, things began to change in my favor again. My financial life improved, but most importantly my spiritual life changed for the better as well.

My strained relationship with my wife was, for the first time in years, on the mend. Because I lived a life with an adopted money philosophy, I had no real measure of how to handle my own catastrophic financial events when they occurred. The adopted money system then spilled over into the other most important parts of my life - my relationship with God, Kathleen and our five children. So give up excuses. If things do not turn out the way you expect them to, ask your inner self, "What were my beliefs about that event? What did I do to create that result in my life? What do I need to do differently next time?" And, "What do I want to occur next?" The following are some ways to better handle future events:

- Acknowledge your current negative views toward money.
- Stop complaining about past money decisions that ended poorly.
- If you have a legitimate complaint with someone regarding a money decision, take it to those who can affect change. Don't complain to those who are powerless.
- Replace complaints about your money with requests for change or take action to affect change.

- Realize you are not the victim. Acknowledge that your money actions or inactions caused your current financial situation.
- Take ownership in knowing that today's money outcome is the result of money choices you made yesterday and in the past.
- Stop blaming others for your money troubles and take ownership of your own money philosophy.

"All blame is a waste of time. No matter how much fault you find with another, and regardless of how much you blame him, it will not change you." - Wayne Dyer

3. Be Purpose Driven About What You Want Your Money to Do for You

We have all been told over and over again on television, in books and on the World Wide Web that we have purpose. Well, I guess I am going to sound like a broken record here. We do have purpose. So to help you find your positive money philosophy, it is important to understand the purpose behind your money. With purpose or your *why* factor, your money will take on a new meaning. You will begin to see that with a money philosophy resource, opportunities and even other successful people will begin to move toward you. Consider the statements below when thinking of developing your positive money philosophy and finding your billionaire within.

- "You are not here to merely make a living. You are here to enable the world to live more amply, with greater vision, with a finer spirit of hope and achievement. You are here to enrich the world, and you impoverish yourself if you forget the errand." – Woodrow Wilson
- "Money is only a tool. It will take you wherever you wish, but it will not replace you as the driver." - Ayn Rand
- "No matter what you've done for yourself or for humanity, if you can't look back on having given love and attention to your own family, what have you really accomplished?" - Lee Iacocca
- "Success is the peace of mind achieved when you know – in your heart – that you did your best at maximizing your potential according to your values. It has little to do with what others think of you." – Darvin Raph
- "I was worth about over a million dollars when I was 23 and over ten million dollars when I was 24, and over a hundred million dollars when I was 25 and… it wasn't that important - because I never did it for the money." – Steve Jobs

Discovering your purpose will be a major driving factor in keeping you on your financial track in life's journey. Being purpose driven means you are doing what you truly love to do and accomplishing what is truly important to you. When you establish purpose it is easy to decide what you want your money to do for you, you're family and even your philanthropic desires. Those who have been truly successful in fulfilling their life's purpose usually found that financial success shadows its purpose. I believe that success follows the wealthy because all of their activities track closely behind a purpose driven lifestyle. I do not necessarily endorse some of the lifestyle decisions of wealthy individuals, but when you track the common money behaviors, you can find a pattern of success and map one for yourself. Committing to a laser-focused, purpose driven life will allow you set the tone and stage for what you decide to do with your wealth.

"While money can't buy happiness, it certainly lets you choose your own form of misery." - Groucho Marx

4. Decide What You Want Your Money to Do for You

Another key reason why most people have not developed a positive money philosophy is because they have not decided what they want financially. They simply have not defined or acknowledged their money desires in a clear and cohesive manner. Jack Canfield, bestselling author of *The Success Principles*, said this mindset of not knowing what we want starts in early childhood development. Canfield said we are trained at a very young age by parents, teachers, coaches and other role models to simply not ask for what we want with verbal responses like:

- Don't touch that.
- Keep your hands off that.

- You don't really feel that way.
- Eat everything on your plate whether you like it or not.

As we grow older we hear:

- You can't have everything you want simply because you want it.
- Money doesn't grow on trees.
- Stop doing what you're doing and come do what I want you to do.

As a result, according to Canfield and what I can attest to from my experiences both personally and professionally, we end up doing what others want us to do with our lives and professions, even our money. We become callous to our own money wants and desires. To avoid this trap, take small, achievable steps when developing a wants plan versus a traditional needs plan for your financial life. Make it part of your overall positive money philosophy. I suggest you get out some paper and a pen. Start jotting down some of these thoughts then Decide, Commit & Execute! ™

- Make a list of wants; what you desire for your financial life. Commit to investing time here. You want to get to the core of your money desires.
- Write out the goals you have for your life. Do not worry about the *how* just yet; focus on what you want in your lifetime.

- Make sure the financial dreams and goals you have are yours not someone else's.
- Define your ideal financial life intertwined with work, career, home, health, fitness, relationships and your spiritual life.
- Share your dreams and goals with someone you trust, so they can encourage and support you along the way.

"One reason so few of us achieve what we truly want is that we never direct our focus; we never concentrate our power. Most people dabble their way through life, never deciding to master anything in particular." – Tony Robbins

5. Believe In the Possibilities of a Positive Money Philosophy

It may sound corny or cliché, but if you want to experience true financial success and the reality of seeing your wants and desires fulfilled financially, you have to believe! In order to develop a positive money philosophy you have to grow your attitude of belief. Science and research has indicated, and in many cases proved, that with positive visualization and proper coaching, training and practice you can accomplish almost anything. You must find that inner belief system that says, "Anything I want is possible."

In my own life, I believe God has aligned the universe for my success. I believe He has also done that for you. Here's the catch:

we must discover and continually arm ourselves with positive affirmations to combat the enemy of our own limited self-beliefs so the billionaire within can rise up. Known for his best-selling book commissioned by Andrew Carnegie, *Think and Grow Rich,* Napoleon Hill said, "You can be anything you want to be, if only you believe with sufficient conviction and act in accordance with your faith; for whatever the mind can conceive and believe the mind can achieve."

According to a June 2000 article on Forbes.com written by Matthew Herper, some of America's wealthiest men never set foot in college. John Simplot for example made billions when he patented the frozen French fry and eventually struck a deal with McDonald's. His children and grandchildren now own the business, J.R. Simplot Co., and are benefiting from a positive money philosophy that started with the "Spud King." Herper went on to talk about the story of Alan Gerry, a high school dropout turned billionaire, who built the first cable television network in upstate New York 10 years after he quit school.

Now, I am not suggesting that an education is not important because it is vital. Gerry went on to study at Dellahany University in New York City where he trained to be an electrician. He took college courses in marketing and administration too. Although he never earned a formal degree, his training shaped his money beliefs and built his business confidence. What was *special* about these billionaires is also buried deep within each one of us - an unwavering belief in themselves and the burning desire and ambition to succeed regardless of how hard the task may seem. Here are some tips to improve your money beliefs:

- The choice in what you believe money can do for you are simply up to you.
- Lose the phrase "I can't."
- Empower your money philosophy with a winning attitude and allow that winning attitude to creep into other areas of your life including your family, work, and spiritual life.
- Do not concern yourself with what others think about you; it is none of your business.
- Base your money beliefs and philosophy around what you want and desire, not what others desire for you.

"There is a secret psychology to money. Most people don't know about it. That's why most people never become financially successful. A lack of money is not the problem; it is merely a symptom of what's going on inside you." - T. Harv Eker

6. Commit to a Positive Money Awareness

In reading this book so far, have you clearly decided and committed to what you want? Do you wholeheartedly believe it is possible to achieve? Do you believe you deserve to have a better financial life? Are you still asking yourself, "OK, what now?"

Well the truth is, so many people exit the train of success before it ever arrives at the station. Trains are so much like the motion of financial success. It takes early energy, effort and time to get a train moving, but once in motion momentum takes over and it is almost impossible to stop. Don't jump off the financial train once you get it moving. The hardest part of the trip is over. Stay on board until you reach your financial destination. The opportunity for success awaits a commitment to your money philosophy. You have to be willing to pay the price for admission in order to fulfill your desires within your money philosophy. Before you can be completely committed, I believe you have to be aware of your limiting beliefs. They will creep back in your mind when you least expect it, sabotage your opportunity for success and impede the development of your positive money philosophy. Most often, limited beliefs about money come from past childhood experiences, friends and even well-meaning family members.

Bob Proctor, the author of *The Power to Have it All,* said "You must begin to understand, therefore, that the present state of your bank account, your sales, your health, your social life, your position at work, etc., is nothing more than the physical manifestation of your previous thinking. If you sincerely wish to change or improve your results in the physical world, you must change your thoughts, and you must change them immediately."

Commit to facing and challenging your limiting money beliefs. Exercise your mind with empowering thoughts and positive affirmations. Here are few tips that helped me fight my own limiting money beliefs:

- Write them down. Acknowledge they exist.
- Write a statement that provokes change in your mind's eye about your negative money philosophy. Dispute and challenge the limited money belief.
- Formulate a new belief or written statement that affirms your new positive money philosophy.
- Keep the new statements in writing at your desk, on your refrigerator or, like my wife does for us, on the mirror in your master bath or family room. It will be a daily reminder and encourage positive money beliefs.

"If you don't put a value on money and seek wealth, you most probably won't receive it. You must seek wealth for it to seek you. If no burning desire for wealth arises within you, no wealth will arise around you. Having definiteness of purpose for acquiring wealth is essential for its acquisition." - Dr. John Demartini

7. Execute Your Positive Money Philosophy

The 7th core principle in developing a positive money philosophy cannot be completed without properly executing steps one through six. To execute a money philosophy and reach our maximum wealth potential, we have to learn how to set SMARTER goals.

Napoleon Hill said, "Every human being who reaches the age of understanding of the purpose of money, wishes for it. Wishing will not bring riches. But *desiring* riches with a state of mind that becomes an obsession, then planning definite ways and means to acquire riches, and backing those plans with persistence *which does not recognize failure*, will bring riches."

I am giving you what I believe Hill meant in his statement; believing is being SMARTER. Set **s**pecific, **m**easurable, **a**ttainable, **r**ealistic and **t**ime-sensitive goals that you **e**valuate and **r**epeat. Please forgive my feeble attempt at trying to make a sentence work with a mnemonic device. I recommend using this simple acronym to cement a successful, powerful, fulfilling and positive money philosophy in your mind.

SMARTER:

- **Specific** money goals are precise and clear. Vague goals yield vague results. A specific goal identifies who is involved, what you want to accomplish, where it must be done and when it should be performed.
- **Measurable** goals are quantifiable. Write the goal out in detail.
  I want $50,000 in my savings account by April 1, 2016. I will achieve this by depositing at least $1,400 a month in my savings account.
- **Achievable** goals must meet the common sense test. You will need to be open to changing your current money

behaviors. Be careful not to limit your beliefs. Increase your money beliefs by expanding your vision of what's possible. Developing your positive mindset, sharpening your current abilities and being open to learning new skills can help you stay on track to achieve your positive money philosophy.

- **Realistic** goals are about keeping it real. You have to be willing and able to work. Stay focused on your money goal by keeping it closely connected to your overall positive money purpose. Remember to stretch your limits.

- **Time-sensitive** goals have an end date that can be marked on the calendar. A sense of urgency helps squash the pro-crastination monster.

- **Evaluate** and **Repeat** your positive money philosophy using the SMARTER money goals. Doing so is the insur-ance policy on opportunity to attain financial success.

"Goals are the fuel in the furnace of achievement."
- Brian Tracy

3

Why Do I Need to Transition to a Positive Money Philosophy?

"For the past 33 years, I have looked in the mirror every morning and asked myself: 'If today were the last day of my life, would I want to do what I am about to do today?' And whenever the answer has been 'No' for too many days in a row, I know I need to change something." - Steve Jobs

If you need information in society today, look no further than the search bar on your web browser. The financial industry is spending millions advertising to a hungry, data-gathering audience. Information is readily at our fingertips. Unfortunately, more information comes with more confusion and less comprehension. If everyone understood the information they attained, wouldn't credit card debt, foreclosures and bankruptcies decline rather than rise?

Whatever financial philosophy Americans have adopted is clearly not working. So what is needed? I believe a personally developed, positive money philosophy integrated with a process-driven approach to wealth mastery is the only answer. To truly transition to a new money philosophy, you have to give up sacred money beliefs and challenge what you previously believed to be true regarding your money decisions. As a financial advisor, I found that those who had great financial products, but little to no financial process had a higher degree of falling short on their wealth goals.

While it takes financial products/instruments to implement a financial process, the products should not be the primary focus. Your focus should be to first identify your own positive money philosophy and then seek to align it with your financial process of wealth mastery. It is also crucial to find advisors who will focus on the financial process over the investment product.

In the following chapters we will examine six common financial instruments that you, as a consumer, will use or be exposed to financially at some point in your life. Before I breakdown these six instruments and how they need to align with your money philosophy, I want you to know the rules we all have to play by in our current financial system. When you more clearly understand the rules and the game board on which you play, then, and only then, will you have the chance to transition from novice to master of your positive money philosophy.

The Financial Game Board

"I think it's wrong that only one company makes the game Monopoly." - Steven Wright

For those of you old enough to relate, do you remember when we were first introduced to the board game Monopoly? It is still one of my all-time favorite strategy games. If by the rare chance you have never played, I highly encourage and recommend you do so especially if you have children. Monopoly is a great early lesson in money principles and money strategy. In my early experience and understanding of the game, my focus and goal was to simply get around the board without landing in jail to collect my $200 for passing Go. As my knowledge and awareness increased, money philosophies began to develop. I learned that buying real estate, owning stock in utilities and building a railroad was more important than just passing Go and collecting an entitlement. As a sidebar, this is a life lesson that needs to be re-examined in our society today; a future topic I am planning to dive into in my next book - *The Entitlement Generation*. Stay tuned. While playing Monopoly, I learned that the life and money decisions we make are not always easy. The game showed me that challenges could exist along the way. The momentum of the game could shift to another player and I could lose my real estate holdings, be forced to sell my stock, negotiate deals and, in some rare cases, have to admit I was bankrupt and my time in the game had come to an end.

In life, the money decisions we make are not much different than Monopoly, except our financial decisions are real, the risk of loss is greater and the lives of those depending on us to get it right are at stake. When you think about the game board of your financial life, I would guess there are four players - you, corporations, financial companies and the federal government, which is the most powerful of them all. In this financial game, a monopoly of sorts already exists. The other three players have the benefit of setup and design. Your co-players set all the rules and requirements of the game before you ever started to play. They also control the game by being able to change the rules when it benefits them and they do it on a regular basis. They also manipulate the rules by promoting their products through the media and other community outlets. Due to their advantage and overwhelming institutional power, your chance of winning is greatly diminished unless you employ a money philosophy and well disciplined financial strategy to guide you through the game.

My focus and goal in this chapter is to give you my knowledge of the financial game board, along with the requirements and rules I learned through years of mentorship, financial training and research. I hope to show you the potential financial pitfalls that exist on your financial game board and give you a better opportunity to defeat your opponents at their own game. You must understand and apply the new information about the game board to have a chance at winning. Only then will you be able to find and seize opportunities, and manage financial instruments and wealth strategies to maximize your benefit. The outcome should be that your life is more enjoyable and potentially more successful.

The Requirement of Every Financial Institution

"It is well enough that people of the nation do not understand our banking and monetary system, for if they did, I believe there would be a revolution before tomorrow morning."
-Henry Ford

Understanding the rules of the game board you play on is an important component of mastering the game. Since understanding or simply attaining information is not enough to gain financial success, you must know how to maximize the rules for your own benefit. I define financial institutions as banks, credit unions, mutual fund companies, insurance companies and the government. The guidelines by which these institutions operate can be broken down into four simple requirements that we have to follow in order to play the game.

1. Financial institutions require our money to start the game.
2. They want more of it and to keep playing the game, they want it to come in on an ongoing basis.
3. Once we have our money circulating in the game, they want to hold on to it for as long as possible.
4. If and when we request or require money back, the financial institution seeks to give us as little as possible.

Allow me to be clear: I am not suggesting that financial institutions are bad. On the contrary, financial institutions make, design and bring to market all the services and products we need and want to live our daily lives. We do, however, have to understand that these institutions have a clear advantage by knowing how to build their own wealth. Since most of us lack the time to properly research all of our money decisions, we haphazardly allow financial institutions to watch over and care for our money. Doing so gives these institutions the control and flexibility to manipulate your money so they can maximize their benefit. In the following chapters, I will show you six ways you might be giving financial institutions greater control and potentially losing hundreds of thousands, even millions of dollars throughout your life. One of the primary reasons why I developed and created **The Black Box Society**™, was to give consumers access to independent financial information on their own time, so they can truly research, discover and learn the requirements of financial institutions in order to maximize their own wealth potential.

The Rights of Ownership

"People who own property feel a sense of ownership in their future and their society. They study, save, work, strive and vote. And people trapped in a culture of tenancy do not."
- Henry Louis Gates

When playing on the financial game board of life, we have many choices in what we buy and own. The ownership choices on our real life game board can be broken down into three classes - paper assets, real estate and business ownership. Paper assets are comprised of stocks, bonds, mutual funds, stock options, annuities, cash value insurance contracts, or any instrument that an entity or individual issues to document the verification of rights, warrants or ownership. Real estate would be defined as holding a deed or title to a home, condominium, apartment building or commercial property, which includes REITs, real estate investment trusts. Lastly, business ownership would include any entity you have direct ownership of and/or voting rights. Business ownership in the United States can be divided into six commonly used entity structures - sole proprietorship, C corporations, S corporations, general partnerships, limited partnerships and limited liability companies. The type of entity you use should not be a flippant decision. It is important to research and seek competent legal counsel that is well versed in business structures. You should discuss with your attorney the advantages and disadvantages of the entity best suited for your own particular case. If you want detailed information from competent legal experts, stay connected to **The Black Box Society**™.

How an asset is owned can be broken down into two basic categories - non-qualified and qualified assets. Non-qualified assets are assets currently subject to federal, state and local taxes. U.S. tax law defines qualified assets as assets that accumulate on a tax-deferred basis until withdrawn at retirement, which is usually at age 59 ½.

Taxes are usually assessed at the marginal rate that exists when a qualified retirement distribution is taken. These assets are normally recognized as a 401(k), 403(b), SEP, Keogh plan or IRA. Roth IRAs were added to the qualified asset mix in 1997 under the Taxpayer Relief Act. It got its name from its legislative sponsor, Sen. William Roth, of Delaware. The Roth IRA allows post-tax contributions, tax deferrals during the accumulation phase and income tax free withdrawals at age 59 ½. If your plans allows you to withdraw money from qualified accounts before age 59 ½, you will typically incur a 10 percent excise tax plus ordinary income tax. (Roth IRAs would only incur the 10 percent excise tax, as ordinary income tax would have been paid prior to the contribution.) Deciding which category you place an asset in has short- and long-term advantages and disadvantages. Choosing to use a qualified versus non-qualified account for long-term retirement planning greatly depends on what you believe our future taxation will look like and when you start taking distributions. We will discuss the use of qualified and non-qualified assets, and how they should be closely aligned with your money philosophy in the upcoming chapters. It is also discussed in great detail inside **The Black Box Society™**.

The Rules of Engagement

"You have to learn the rules of the game. And then you have to play better than anyone else." - Albert Einstein

What if we did not have financial institutions? Who would design and package financial instruments or products to meet the needs of the public? How could we protect, preserve and grow our money and our assets? Consider what life would look like without insurance companies. We would have to assume all risk in protecting our assets, income and life from unwanted events like premature death, disability, car accidents, home or business loss, theft, fires, lawsuits and countless other wealth eroding factors that exist in our world. Without banks, commerce as we know it would come to a screeching halt. We have all complained about how much banks overcharge or how poorly the banks treat us as consumers. Honestly though, try to imagine living without the services our banks and credit unions provide. Could you imagine a world without depository services, bill pay assistance, or consumer and small business lending? Our financial systems would seize up overnight without the existence of banks. Consider the corporations that make products we use every day. We have the opportunity to trade securities and debts of publicly traded corporations like Apple, Microsoft and Google because of the free trade enterprise that exists in the U.S. I could not run my business without the use of a computer, the internet and my smartphone.

Lastly, we have a need for the largest financial institution of them all - the U.S. government. Our government makes laws to govern society, regulate our money supply, collect taxes to support infrastructure, defend our borders and provide social support for those in need of assistance. We can all agree that there is a great need for the numerous financial institutions with which we have to co-exist. Finding that balance between your positive money philosophy and the services offered by financial institutions will be critical in developing a successful wealth-purposed plan.

"The number one problem in today's generation and economy is the lack of financial literacy." - Alan Greenspan

4

What If What We Knew to Be True About Taxation Changed?

"One thing is clear: The Founding Fathers never intended a nation where citizens would pay nearly half of everything they earn to the government." – Ron Paul

There was an important anniversary in the United States this year. It quietly passed by without making much of a splash in our papers, on television or even in the top Yahoo!, Bing or Google searches. But this quiet anniversary affects, or maybe I should say infects, every household in the United States of America. February 3, 2013 marked the 100th anniversary of the 16th Amendment, which allows Congress to collect income tax. Now you can see why there are no ticker tape parades, no family picnics with the kids dressed in red, white and blue; and why no yellow ribbons are tied around the old oak tree for Uncle Sam.

"Government's view of the economy could be summed up in a few short phrases: If it moves, tax it. If it keeps moving, regulate it. And if it stops moving, subsidize it." – Ronald Reagan

In its early roots, income taxes were supposed to be temporary. But the temporary tax just celebrated its 100th anniversary and Uncle Sam has absolutely no plan to abolish it any time soon. Therefore, there are two early questions about taxation you should consider when developing your positive money philosophy as it relates to taxation.

1. Do you believe that your personal income taxes are going up or down in the future?
2. Do you believe the U.S. government will raise or lower personal income tax in the future?

There are three answers you could give to these two questions, but before you do that let's look at some historical data and current debates to see what they suggest. Your personal money philosophy, as it relates to taxes, will be the major driving force behind what long-term financial decisions you make going forward. You will discover, as you read on, that income tax and other taxes levied against you can erode your future accumulation of wealth. As a matter of fact, many of the taxes you and I pay beyond federal taxes may surprise you.

Get out your cell phone, power, or utility bill to see what these taxes look like in your household. It may not seem like much now, but think about these purchases and the taxes paid on them over your lifetime. Furthermore, many Americans pay these additional taxes unknowingly and rarely, if ever, talk to their tax advisor about the potential deductibility of these additional taxes on their federal income tax returns. The following is a short list showing how our government collects tax revenue to fund entitlement programs, defend our borders and support campaign promises made by our politicians.

Accounts receivable tax; airport tax; building permit tax; business tax; cigarette tax; county tax; cable TV tax; food license tax; hotel tax; inheritance tax; telephone federal universal service fee tax; septic permit tax; sewer tax; telephone usage charge tax; telephone federal excise tax; telephone state and local tax; fuel tax; energy tax, which includes gas, electric, heating and oil; water tax, sewer tax; state tax; city tax; property tax; user taxes; utility tax; marriage license tax; road toll booth tax, corporate income tax; vehicle sales tax, watercraft registration tax, fishing license tax, state tax, personal property tax; long term capital gains tax; short-term capital gains tax; Medicare tax; workers compensation tax; unemployment tax; road usage tax; real estate tax; toll booth tax; hunting license tax; recreational vehicle tax; and health insurance tax.

This by no means is an all-inclusive list, but rather a sampling of some of the most popular ways local, state and federal governments collect revenue from citizens. A large number of these taxes have been around for over a hundred years in duties and tariffs. The government practice of taxing goods, services, assets and income dates back thousands of years to early Egypt, Greece and Rome. Our current tax schemes in the U.S. were influenced primarily by Great Britain and the Roman Empire. We can see these early English and Roman influences in many Americans' largest asset – real estate. When you purchase a piece of real estate, you are granted title to the property by the government. In return, the government says you must pay the levied real estate tax it has assessed in order to keep the title.

Property rights evolved from the feudal system, which viewed the king, his governors and lords to be the technical owner of all land. Today, we most commonly exercise fee simple ownership. Laws grant the property rights individuals are permitted to hold. "Permitted to hold" is the key phrase. Think of the influence feudalism had on taxation as it relates to real estate this way: The king was the federal government and granted rights and powers to his governors, or state governments, which gave lords, or local municipalities, the authority to tax and take land for public use. We will spend more time discussing real estate in detail later in the book. You can also obtain some of the best financially relevant information and tax strategies by going to **The Black Box Society**™ risk-free for 30 days.

"A lot of Americans think they got a tax cut, and they didn't because their local property tax went up, their excise tax went up, their sales tax went up, and their prices went up and everything else, because we failed to invest in some of these other things we ought to be doing. We are squeezing the middle class, we are losing the middle class, and the gap between the haves and the have-nots is growing wider and wider, not closing as it used to be." - John Kerry

Our government is starving for more tax revenue, and the politicians you and I have put in office over the years cannot seem to agree on anything that resembles a balanced budget, not to mention reducing the national deficit that stands at $16.8 trillion and is growing by more than $50,000 per second. It seems inconceivable that our debt could be so high, but it is the unfortunate reality. David Walker, who served as the U.S. Comptroller General from 1998 to 2008, said the national debt is at crisis levels. In his book, *Comeback America,* Walker said America has fiscal cancer that will kill the republic if not treated. He gave a couple of antidotes that could save us from financial demise. He said taxes could be increased by two times what they are today, which means our top rate would skyrocket to over 70 percent and the bottom rate to over 20 percent. Secondly, he said, the president and Congress would have to agree on cutting all mandatory and discretionary spending by more than 50 percent. If I had to guess the poison pill our politicians would pick, it would be to raise taxes. Please refer back to the first two questions at the beginning of this chapter and answer either "Yes, No or Undecided."

I have been verbally polling people since 2008. When asked, "Do you believe income tax rates will go up or go down in future?" almost all said "Yes, I believe taxes are on the rise!" Those who said "No" had a basic economic belief that their current income was so low that they would not be affected one way or the other. For a small group of Americans, this response may be true when you only consider federal income tax. Not only is the federal government starved for revenue, the issues can be seen at the state and local levels too.

If the question was expanded to include every tax, fee, tariff and toll, I believe we would all face the undeniable reality that taxes have to go up. Currently, the growing demands of social security, Medicare, Medicaid, ObamaCare and other mandatory benefit programs make up more than 60 percent of our federal budget and they are projected to grow. Mandatory spending is spending that the government has no direct control over. Our politicians have passed legislation that guarantees benefits to people who qualify for them, known as entitlement programs. Our legislators either have to pay the benefits or change the law. How many of the politicians you voted for have the cojones to demand cuts to social security, Medicare and Medicaid?

The other 40 percent of our federal budget is made up of discretionary spending. Our representatives in Congress have full discretion over this type of spending. It consists of spending for line items such as defense, national security, roads, the environment, justice, and money circulation. Well, to be accurate, I should also include anything your political advocate can think of for their state or district. Walker goes on to tell us in *Comeback America* that by 2040, according to budget simulations, our federal tax revenues will only be enough to cover the interest on our national debt, Medicare and Medicaid. Everything else, including social security and national defense, will not be funded.

Walker is not alone in his beliefs regarding the looming financial storm in America. Laurence Kotlikoff, who is an economics professor at Boston University and author of *The Coming Generational Storm* and *Spend 'Til the End,* has similar predictions. In 2004, Kotlikoff said we would face skyrocketing tax rates, lower savings, high inflation, high unemployment and a rapidly depreciating dollar by 2030. Almost ten years have passed since he sounded the alarm and little to no action has been taken in making a change. He went on to say that many of us have predicted our tax planning on one single assumption; that we will be in a lower tax bracket in the future. With that in mind, we are urged to save as much as possible in pre-tax plans, such as IRAs and 401(k) accounts. The topic of potentially toxic qualified plans will be discussed in detail in the following chapters. Conventional financial wisdom says that by deferring your taxes today, your trade-off will be lower taxes tomorrow. The tax cuts that many of us have enjoyed since 2001 began creeping back at the end of 2012.

As of January 1, 2013, every American employee went back to work after the holidays only to experience a belated Christmas gift from Uncle Sam. He gave us all a 2 percent increase in payroll taxes by ending the payroll tax holiday. It was part of the Tax Relief Act of

2010 and it took us back to the default payroll tax rate of 6.2 percent. The payroll tax you pay does not include the additional 6.2 percent your employer contributes to social security on your behalf. Every American employee and employer contributes a collective total of 15.3 percent to social security and Medicare, respectively. The breakdown of your payroll deductions and your employer contributions looks like this:

- Social Security – Employee payroll deduction 6.2%
- Social Security – Employer matches additional 6.2%
- Medicare – Employee payroll deduction 1.45%
- Medicare – Employer matches additional 1.45%

When you consider payroll tax, in addition to state and local taxes, and our current progressive federal income tax system, as illustrated below, you can understand why I believe it is imperative to consider any legal and legitimate strategy that could reasonably reduce your taxable income today and tomorrow.

You do not want to just postpone taxes like most uninformed financial advisors or product-driven salespeople have a tendency to do. There are four federal income tax filing classifications you could fall into - single, married filing jointly or qualifying widow(er), married filing separately and head of household. For illustration purposes, I only used the married filing jointly/qualifying widow(er) schedule. Additional tax rate information and schedules can be found at www.irs.gov.

FEDERAL MARGINAL INCOME TAX RATES FOR 2013

Marginal Tax Rate	Single	Married Filing Jointly or Qualified Widow(er)	Married Filing Separately	Head of Household
10%	$0 – $8,925	$0 – $17,850	$0 – $8,925	$0 – $12,750
15%	$8,926 – $36,250	$17,851 – $72,500	$8,926 – $36,250	$12,751 – $48,600
25%	$36,251 – $87,850	$72,501 – $146,400	$36,251 – $73,200	$48,601 – $125,450
28%	$87,851 – $183,250	$146,401 – $223,050	$73,201 – $111,525	$125,451 – $203,150
33%	$183,251 – $398,350	$223,051 – $398,350	$111,526 – $199,175	$203,151 – $398,350
35%	$398,351 – $400,000	$398,351 – $450,000	$199,176 – $225,000	$398,351 – $425,000
39.6%	$400,001+	$450,001+	$225,001+	$425,001+

A growing number of tax experts and economists agree that after all taxes have been considered, middle-class Americans could be losing upwards of 40 percent of their gross income to taxes each year. Imagine if the government decided to increase our federal income tax rates by two times what they are today? We all understand that our government needs tax revenue to survive, but what looms is a feast at the expense of its citizens. If this occurs, it will feel as if the zombie apocalypse has occurred. The government will begin fiscally eating citizens. I suggest you stop procrastinating. Take full responsibility for discovering what "paying your fair share" really means to you and your family. Then, act on the positive money philosophies you learned in chapter two.

> *"No government can exist without taxation. This money must necessarily be levied on the people; and the grand art consists of levying so as not to oppress." - Fredrick the Great*

Cullen Murphy, author of *The New Rome*, pointed out some thought provoking yet unsettling parallels between America and ancient Rome. He pointed to a decline in moral values and civility, an overextended military, border control issues and fiscal irresponsibility of the government as reasons for the fall of Rome. Are those issues eerily familiar to you? They were to me the first time I read it and I started to think about what I could do to make changes in my own house and personal money philosophy. I also started thinking about what I could do to help my country get back on track. It led me to take action in helping and encouraging others to examine their own personal money philosophies. A core strategy to implement your money philosophy should be to design a sound wealth purposed plan that prevents or minimizes the effect of income and other taxes on your future wealth. Here are some actions that can help you get a jump-start on planning for future tax explosions in the U.S.:

- Join *The Black Box Society*™. The exclusive member community seeks to uncover the secrets of positive money philosophies and principles as they relate to taxes. Try it risk-free for 30 days.

- Examine your exemptions, withholdings, deductions and tax credits with a tax expert who can help you discover if you are paying more than your fair share.
- Register to vote and exercise your right to vote for fiscally responsible lawmakers.
- Reach out to your elected officials and respectfully voice your tax concerns for our country. Also ask them to provide you with their voting record in reference to fiscal responsibility. Here is a great link to reach your representatives: **http://www.usa.gov/Contact/Elected.shtml**
- Become a local voice of reason for fiscal responsibility with your locally elected officials.
- Take full responsibility for your own tax minimization planning and other financial affairs. Forget about postponing taxes; minimize them.
- Only work with expert tax advisors who share your concern and have strategies for the looming tax storm.
- Make sure the seven core principles of a positive money philosophy are implemented with your overall wealth plan and investments.

"When the federal government spends more each year than it collects in tax revenues, it has three choices: It can raise taxes, print money, or borrow money. While these actions may benefit politicians, all three options are bad for average Americans." - Ron Paul

5

How My 401(k) Account Could Bankrupt Me

"The trick is to stop thinking of it as 'your' money." - IRS auditor

Early in my career as an investment advisor, I spent much of my time in client meetings discussing retirement planning and the financial instruments that are most often used to fund retirement accounts. An overwhelming majority of my clients owned some variation of a 401(k) or qualified pre-tax retirement account. It could have been a SIMPLE IRA, 403(b) Tax-Sheltered Annuity, Simplified Employee Pension, Keogh, Thrift Savings Plan, pension or profit-sharing plan. It really didn't matter. My clients' believed they were saving money in the most efficient way possible to meet a future financial need. For simplicity sake, I will refer to all of these qualified plans under the umbrella of a 401(k). As time passed and I became more ingrained in the financial services industry, I was shocked to find that people knew very little, as did a large number of financial advisors.

I became keenly aware that most people were just trying to do the right thing. They wanted to save for worthwhile goals, but were just financially uneducated about how to do it in the most effective and efficient way. All they knew was that they needed to be saving for retirement and that the 401(k) was the easiest way since it was deducted right from their paycheck.

The financial services industry, its advisors and large corporations knew this too, so they began to pour hundreds of millions of dollars into marketing the benefits of a 401(k), calling it a great employee benefit. To examine how this phenomenon with 401(k) s occurred, you have to start with a guy named Ted Benna. Ted Benna grew up on a Pennsylvania dairy farm and later became an expert pension consultant who advised large corporations. If you retired from a large corporation in the '60s and '70s, you would receive a pension. Benna would help set those plans up, but he was bored and unhappy with the same old pension plan design and greedy executives. Then in 1978, he stumbled across an obscure addition to the tax code passed by Congress – Section 401, sub paragraph k.

The 401(k) started out as an unassuming tax break for corporations that would let the employee sock cash away on the side into two simple and straightforward funds. One day it hit Benna between the eyes. If employers would add a match to their employee's contribution, he realized it would incentivize the employee to participate and give the employer an additional tax break. Benna believed that the 401(k) plan would take off and indeed it did. In 1979, Johnson & Johnson became an early player in the process of adopting a 401(k). By the end of 1984, over 17,000 companies had followed suit. The rise of the 401(k) had taken place at the expense and demise of the great American pension plan.

According to the Employee Benefit Research Institute, active participants were just shy of 8 million in 1984 and total assets had reached $91 billion. By 1990, the number of active participants had climbed to 19.5 million with $384 billion in assets. Fast-forward to 2012, the total number of American workers contributing to 401(k) plans is said to be over 51 million, representing approximately $3.5 trillion in assets. It has been 34 years since Benna fathered the creation of the 401(k), but what's the rest of the story you ask? I believe the rest of the story is what you believe to be true about your financial future both from a micro and macroeconomic view. First and foremost, you need to consider what you believe your future income taxes and global taxes will look like when you start taking distributions from your plan. Consider the number of financial institutions, advisors, coworkers, family members and friends that will tell you how much to contribute, what to buy and where to invest your 401(k) contributions. Hardly anyone has a tax minimization exit strategy. All of the focus is put on dumping money into the plan with little to no concentration on how to get it out.

The misperception with a 401(k) plan is that you will save taxes when you make a pre-tax contribution to your plan. Let's examine this notion. A pre-tax savings plan does not save on taxes; it simply postpones the tax. Therefore, if you believe that your personal income tax in the future could be higher than what it is today, you should reconsider how much tax you postpone. Do not be fooled into believing it is an income-tax savings in any year you contribute money to a 401(k). You have only deferred payment of the inevitable tax to a future time. But in all likelihood, a potentially higher tax rate faces you and me in the future, based on the irrational expenditures and mandatory spending our society and government has committed us to.

Beyond the concept of thinking that you save on taxes by making contributions to a 401(k) is the notion that when you retire, you will be in a lower tax bracket because you will be making less money. When you are in retirement, you will need to consider possibly having other income sources that will be counted toward your taxable income. You should also consider that many of your deductible expenses, such as home mortgage interest, business expenses and deductions for children, will be gone, creating additional taxes. Lastly, you need to consider that the largest institution of them all - the U.S. government - makes the rules for your 401(k). If it needs more tax revenue, what better place to get it than from an account that has never been taxed? It is as if the government, financial institutions, media, friends and even well meaning family members have preprogrammed us for financial failure. Be careful when developing a positive money philosophy, as it relates to 401(k) contributions and distributions.

Do not be duped into thinking you will be in a lower tax bracket when you retire by contributing to a 401(k). Blindly trusting the money philosophy that says you will save taxes today and defer your income tax to a lower tax bracket is unsafe and reckless. It is not your fault, but you have to take responsibility for your actions. The media and most financial advisors claim there is a tax savings that will pad your pocket when you contribute savings to a qualified plan. So let's examine the example below to discover what is actually true.

Assumptions

Person "A"	Person "B"
Earns: $100,000 a year	Earns: $100,000 year.
401(k) contribution: $15K	401(k) contribution: $0.00
MTB*: 25%	MTB*: 25%
Tax Owed: $21,250	Tax Owed: $25,000
Net: $63,750	Net: $75,000
Net Difference: $0.00	Net Difference: $11,250 after tax

*Marginal Tax Bracket

If we compare person "A" to person "B," we can see they make the same amount of money and are therefore in the same marginal tax bracket. The only difference between the two is "A" chose to put $15,000 in his 401(k) because he was under the assumption that he would experience $3,750 in tax savings. You can see that "A" netted $63,750 after taxes and that his $15,000 contribution is inside the 401(k) account, but where are the tax savings for person "B?" Look closely at the taxes owed by person "A" and person

"B". Person "A" owes $3,750 less in taxes than person "B," but person "B" netted $11,250 more after taxes. Wondering where the tax savings are for person "A?" They are inside the plan.

Think of it this way, inside the plan you own $11,250 and the IRS owns $3,750 for a total of $15,000. The tax savings are in the plan with your money. It would seem that this is obvious, but many advisors and media hawks still claim those who make a contribution to their 401(k) have the tax savings to use again before retirement.

If you're still not sure of yourself think of it like this; if you were allowed to contribute your entire paycheck, say $100,000, to your plan, you would have no money to pay bills. It's true that you would pay $25,000 less in taxes than person "B," but you would not have the tax savings in your current cash flow. It would all be inside the plan with your other $75,000. You would be virtually bankrupt, but you would have $100,000 locked up in your 401(k) account at the same time. If you have a financial advisor or tax expert counting this perceived tax savings, consider handing them a copy of my book or ask them to download it. Look at it like this; an investment of $20 or less for my book could save both of you hundreds of thousands in retirement.

Now consider your financial future. If Congress introduces and passes new tax laws and directs the IRS to adjust all marginal tax brackets upwards by two times what they are today, 10 percent becomes 20 percent at the bottom and 39.6 percent becomes 79 percent at the top. If you do not believe it is possible, just look back at our tax history to get a peak at what our future could hold. When income tax was first introduced in 1913, the lowest brackets paid only 1 percent, while the top bracket paid 7 percent, respectively. By 1944, just 31 short years later, the bottom bracket was up to 23 percent and the top bracket had skyrocketed to 91 percent.

Imagine for a moment your 401(k) was around in 1913 and you were encouraged to contribute a portion of your paycheck to the company retirement plan. Let's assume you were in the middle bracket at 3 percent and that you also assumed you would retire to the lowest bracket of 1 percent 31 years later. Flash forward to your retirement party. One of your coworkers turns on the radio to liven the party with a little music, but normal programming has been canceled for a special news report. Congress has just passed the Individual Income Tax Act of 1944. Suddenly, with the stroke of a pen, your tax rate just went from 3 percent to a whopping low rate of 23 percent! That was a 667 percent increase in your taxes overnight, or what I would refer to as inevitable bankruptcy if you were planning on a 1 percent tax rate at retirement. It seems like an extreme example, but that was reality in 1944. Could that happen again?

In chapter 4 numerous tax experts including David Walker, the former government accountability office chief, and brilliant economists, like Laurence Kotlikoff, will speak to why they believe hyper taxation and inflation is not outside the realm of possibilities in the next 15 to 20 years. Due to your limited liquidity, use and control over 401(k) accounts, the risk of bankruptcy in retirement could be more of a reality than any of us want to imagine. You have to take personal responsibility and implement a positive money philosophy to mitigate any future tax explosions that could impact retirement plans.

Hopefully I have your attention. But are you still skeptical because your employer pays you to put money in their plan? Some employers match the contributions of their employees, sometimes dollar for dollar. If you are receiving a match from your employer, it is valuable and certainly adds to the overall equation of participating in a plan. Just remember the disadvantages of a pretax retirement plan without a match when deciding whether to contribute money to a qualified pretax retirement plan like a 401(k).

Here is the problem with matching contributions, as I have seen it presented over the last 20 years. Many people think they get a 50 percent return on their money when an employer matches 50 percent of the employee contribution. But what you perceive to be true is not always reality. Allow me to explain before you slam the book shut or turn off your device. Let's say you contributed $10,000 to your plan and your employer rewarded your contribution with .50 cents for every dollar you contributed up to $10,000. The total amount in your 401(k) account would now be $15,000. "What could be better Kenny?" "I just got a 50 percent return on my money? I think you are dead wrong."

OK, give me two more minutes to explain. If you had immediate access to the money then you would be right and I would be wrong. The problem is your 401(k) requires the money stay in the plan until you reach the required minimum retirement age. There is a gap between the time that the matching contribution is made and when you can take it out. In that gap of time, your money and the employer's match are exposed to investment risk, as well as future taxation. Let's say you faithfully contributed $10,000 to your plan for 31 years and the stock market was kind to you during this period, giving you a generous return of 5 percent. Your account would be worth $520,091.81, of which $310,000 was your money. Now, let's add your employer's equally faithful match of $5,000 for 31 years. Remember, the employer's match to your account that appeared to be a 50 percent return also only earned 5 percent for 31 years. The result - your account returned an effective yield of 7.10 percent for 31 years, making the total value with the employer's match $780,137.71. The employer's match of $5,000 per year at a 5 percent return gave you another $260,045.90 by the end of your 31 years of service. If you were truly getting a 50 percent return on your employer's match, the value at the end of 31 years would have been $2,876,255,888.49. (Your money, growing at 5 percent equals $520,091.81, plus $2,876,255,888.49 from your employer equals a grand total of $3.4 billion dollars.)

If you believe your 50 percent match is a 50 percent return, open up your statements and look for that money result. It should be a big number that is hard to miss. Unfortunately, our perceptions of money truths are sometimes skewed by inaccurate information from well-intended people. Obviously, it would be better to have a match than not, by proof in the more realistic example above that showed an improvement in the overall rate of return by 2.1 percent over 31 years. The fact of the matter is your employer's match to your account is exposed to the same risk associated with investment returns, potential hyper taxation and inflation.

Here are some tips to help you in your journey to discovering your money philosophy as it relates to the potential eroding factors of retirement accounts:

- Cement in your mind that 401(k)s and traditional IRAs do not save taxes; they simply postpone the tax.
- Consider the many personal advantages and disadvantages of 401(k) retirement planning as it relates to your *own* positive money philosophy, not someone else's or that of the financial institution.
- Take a balanced approach to saving. Consider the strategy of your financial process over the financial product when considering your numerous financial choices.
- If you qualify, consider blending Roth 401(k) and Roth IRA products with your traditional qualified retirement planning products.
- Hire a Wealth Coach at Kenneth Porter & Company, Ltd. or work with your own trusted advisor who can help you navigate your financial journey. Make sure their money philosophy and purpose is aligned with yours.

- Remember to have an equally important, if not more important, exit strategy to get the money out of your qualified plan in retirement.
- Take action now. Become a founding member of The Black Box Society™ to discover secret financial strategies that are successfully implemented by other well-informed middle-class Americans.

"As far as your personal goals are and what you actually want to do with your life, it should never have to do with the government. You should never depend on the government for your retirement, your financial security, for anything. If you do, you're screwed." - Drew Carey

6

How Can I Truly Become King of My Own Castle?

"The home to everyone is to him his castle and fortress, as well for his defense against injury and violence, as for his repose." - Edward Coke

Regardless of your income or financial status in society, the home has always been considered a sanctuary. It is viewed as our castle of protection and the basis of early wealth creation. For most of us, it represents the largest asset on our personal balance sheet. Most financial advisors agree and I concur, real estate should be one of the first investments you make. Most people accomplish this when they buy their first home. Congratulations if you are already a homeowner. You took a crucial step in achieving wealth for you and your family.

In this chapter we will examine how to truly take financial control of your castle instead of relinquishing control to the financial institutions. I think it is important to note early on that I have never seen a financial decision, or product, create more emotional upheaval than those decisions regarding real estate. Based on that experience, I am going to ask you in advance to consider the realties involved in your real estate decisions. Have an open mind regarding what I am about to share with you.

When you consider all of the costs involved with the purchase of real estate, it is no wonder consumers become very protective and sensitive regarding their real estate purchase and equity management. When purchasing real estate you have to consider the costs of real estate taxes, mortgage interest, insurance, improvements, power, gas, water, sewage, municipal services and a plethora of other maintenance costs. The sum of these costs could represent millions of dollars over the course of your lifetime. Much of this is unavoidable, but the one expense that usually creates the most stress, both financially and emotionally, is the cost to finance the real estate purchase. How you choose to finance your castle will set in motion either unnecessary wealth erosion, or it will represent one of the greatest opportunities to create wealth over your lifetime.

In chapter 3 we discussed defining your positive money philosophy. I shared with you the requirements of financial institutions and what was necessary to know when playing on the financial game board. When it comes to your mortgage decisions, you should understand how your money works within a mortgage both from a personal micro and macroeconomic point of view. It is important to avoid the long-term devastating costs of the ill-advised mortgage savings promotions that financial institutions, specifically mortgage lenders, occasionally release. While reading this chapter, you will discover that some of the information seems counterintuitive to what you have been taught and led to believe. The black box money philosophy you should consider when it comes to how you should mortgage your property is this: How you decide to pay for your home will directly impact your financial success and overall wealth mastery.

If you finance your home, you are paying interest to the financial institution for the right or privilege of using their money. On the other hand, if you pay cash for your real estate, you will save on interest costs you would have otherwise paid to the financial institution. However, you also lose money because the cash used to purchase the property can no longer earn interest. This is referred to as an opportunity cost. The New Oxford American Dictionary defines opportunity cost as, "the loss of potential gain from other alternatives when one alternative is chosen." When we choose one mortgage product over another, we should consider the opportunity cost. I believe there are seven questions middle-class Americans should ask themselves when seeking out the best positive money philosophy and making a mortgage decision.

1. Why would I have a mortgage at all if I could pay cash?
2. Do I have enough money saved to pay cash for the house I want?
3. Would tax deductions on mortgage interest paid to the lender really matter for me if I took out a mortgage?
4. Could I potentially earn a return in the gap between my interest cost and my interest earned?

5. Do I really understand the impact of inflation, taxes and opportunity costs on my real estate when deciding on how to finance it?
6. Would my house be a good place to leave my capital if I could pay cash?
7. What will my heirs do with my house when I am gone?

Your answers to these seven questions will define your money philosophy. My answers to these seven questions will hopefully help you define a positive money philosophy and how it relates to your mortgage decisions. Here are the facts as I have seen them play out over my professional financial career:

1. Most middle-class Americans cannot pay cash for their home. They simply do not have that luxury. Paying cash for your home is actually the most expensive way to acquire real estate.
2. Middle-class Americans with enough money to pay cash for a home usually find that the money is locked in their 401(k) or nonqualified account that would require them to sell stock and pay taxes. Most choose to avoid that additional cost to acquire property.
3. If you are a middle-class individual or married taxpayer, your phase out exemptions in 2013 will be $250,000 for single taxpayers and $300,000 for married taxpayers filing jointly. In other words, it makes sense for at least 97 percent of Americans who make less than $300,000 a year

to consider having a conversation with their trusted advisor about mortgage interest deductions on personal residences and investment properties.

4. If your goal is to outperform your mortgage interest cost after tax deductions over a long period of time, consider financing your real estate with a fixed mortgage for 30 years instead of 15. Save the difference in a side account to earn more than the tax cost of the mortgage interest and other deductible expenses.

5. Consider inflation when paying down your mortgage. Your first mortgage payment will actually be the most expensive payment and respectively, your last payment will be the cheapest. For example, a $750 monthly payment today could feel like a $458.22 monthly payment in 15 years and a $279.95 payment in 30 years.

6. If you could pay cash for your property, meditate on the fact that your cash payment also comes at a cost of money. You will lose the opportunity for that cash to earn its highest rate of return in an investment or savings account. Let's assume you could earn a net after tax return of 5 percent on your cash for 30 years, and that you just liquidated your side account to pay for your $225,000 house. The true cost of paying cash for your $225,000 home over the 30-year period would be $972,437.

7. Fast forward 30 to 45 years. You are now in the golden years of retirement living in the $972,437 castle you paid for with cash. Unfortunately, you are now facing Father Time and an aging body. Your home is paid for and has been for more

than 30 years, but the Grim Reaper knocked on your door before you could enjoy the wealth buried in your home. Everyone loved and adored you, but when all the tears dry and the emotional toll of your loss is paid, your last will and testament will be read. In a blink of an eye your heirs will likely sell the castle you called home and turn it into cash. Enjoy the peace of mind that comes with having the liquidity, use and control to pay off the home when you choose instead of giving the financial institution complete control.

You may be asking yourself how you can have the liquidity, use and control over your mortgage. First, simply understand what you can afford. Then, look for properties that match your wants within the parameters of what you can afford. You should also consider property taxes, insurance and other ownership costs when considering what you can afford. You should then decide what mortgage product best suits your money philosophy, considering your short- and long-term mortgage objectives. What you know to be true, or hear to be true, may not always be the case or in your best interest. Consider taking the option of a 30-year mortgage over a 15-year mortgage. In contrast, most banks and mortgage lenders lean toward the 15-year mortgage option over 30 years because they want to have liquidity, use and control over your money instead of you. The lenders will often tell us through advertising that paying a 15-year mortgage is less expensive than a 30-year mortgage. It is true that you will pay less interest with a 15-year mortgage, but when you consider all the variables and a reasonable rate of return, a 15-year mortgage actually ends up being more expensive than the 30-year option.

Many consumers fail to consider their after tax costs of the mortgage when comparing the cost of a 15-year mortgage to that of a 30-year mortgage. Let's look at the cost of a 15-year mortgage at 4.25 percent and a 30-year mortgage at 4.75 percent on a $250,000 home. We will also assume that the homeowner is in a 25 percent federal bracket and believes their investments will return 8 percent before taxes over the next 30 years.

Assumptions

15-Year Mortgage	30-Year Mortgage
$250,000 loan amount	$250,000 loan amount
4.25% interest rate	4.75% interest rate
180 payments	360 payments
$1,880.70 P & I	$1,304.12 P & I
8% ROR	8% ROR
25% tax bracket	25% tax bracket

Most financial institutions typically stop the conversation at the amount of total interest you paid on a 15-year mortgage, which in the example above would be $88,535.28 at the end of year 15. However, at the end of year 30, using the 30-year mortgage, you paid $219,482.60 of cumulative interest. It would seem like the bank was right because you spent \$130,947.32 more in interest with the 30-year mortgage than the 15-year option. So why would you want to have a 30-year mortgage in your money philosophy?

Let's look at the rest of the numbers. Since you pay less interest in 15 years versus 30 years, the amount of loan interest that is deductible on your individual tax return will also be less. This simply means that the government has fewer subsidies to add back to your pocket at the end of each tax year. If you could invest the difference in tax savings at 8 percent, the growth of those tax savings in a 30-year over 15-year period would be significant. If you took the \$576.58 difference in monthly payments and include the annual tax savings difference between the two mortgage plans, you would only need to net an after tax return of 4.429 percent to provide a side account of \$167, 660. You would then have liquidity, use and control to pay off your 30-year mortgage if you chose to do so.

So why do consumers fall prey to choosing a 15-year mortgage over a 30-year mortgage, or accelerate their mortgage by prepaying with biweekly payments? It is fairly simple. Their understanding is that a shorter loan term will reduce the cost. Pay cash for your house if you also believe that. Would you be better off with a 15-year mortgage or a 30-year mortgage if faced with a physical disability, premature death, job loss or sequestration? The world is ever-changing, so establish a positive money philosophy that gives you maximum control over your mortgage when change occurs. Make sure it leads to the greatest results and best possible outcome. When you are faced with your next real estate purchase or refinance decision, consider these five questions and tips for financial success:

1. A large down payment or systematic pay downs on my mortgage over time will save me money. True or False?
2. A 15-year mortgage will save me more money over time versus a 30-year mortgage. True or False?
3. I will save money if I make extra payments on my mortgage without considering other financial and emotional factors. True or False?
4. My interest rate is the only factor I need to consider when determining the cost of my mortgage. True or False?
5. I would be more secure having my house paid off rather than financed at or near 100 percent. True or False?

- Consider signing up and taking the *KP&CO 90-Day Wealth Mastery Course*™ to effectively learn how to apply the efficient and effective mortgage strategies to your own positive money philosophy.
- Contact a Wealth Coach at *Kenneth Porter & Company, Ltd.* or your personal trusted advisor that will focus on your wealth-purposed strategy over the needs and wants of a financial institution.

"Get as much of a mortgage as you can for as long as you can. Using someone else's money is always better than using your own." - Ric Edelman

7

What is the Black Box Secret to Compounding My Interest?

"Compound interest is the eighth wonder of the world. He who understands it earns it. He who doesn't pays it." - Albert Einstein

Most consumers have been taught the first sentence in Einstein's quote, but unfortunately many ignore the second half. Understanding the black box secret to compounding interest may become your eighth wonder of the world once you truly understand that the unbridled power of compounding interest could unknowingly erode your wealth. All of our decisions that involve financial products will in some way or another fall back to the magic of compounding interest. In this chapter, I hope to expose you to the dark side of compound interest and the many disadvantages that can occur if you do not know how to mitigate its unintended consequence. I am sure you are asking, "How can compound interest be bad when everyone talks about it being so important to attain wealth?" It is important to refer back to Chapter 3 where we discussed the financial game board and the requirements to play the game. When you play the financial game of compound interest, take note of this unpublished rule: the large print gives and the small print takes away.

Look at any glossy marketing piece printed by a mutual fund and you will quickly see all the wonderful opportunities that specific fund offers you. After close examination, you will see - in very small print - the disclaimers that say something like, "Average annual total return figures include changes in principal value, reinvested dividends, and capital gain distributions. Figures do not include the cost for taxes, capital gain taxes or other expenses." I call this the "gotcha" clause. Now allow me to be clear, I believe most financial institutions are well meaning and provide valuable services to consumers. However, from a marketing point of view the job of the mutual fund distributor is to highlight the good and mitigate the bad. The disclaimer above seems innocent and straightforward at first glance, but when you add the small print the return on investment looks significantly different on paper and in your wallet.

Let's look at an example of compound interest the way most people think of the idea of compounding. So the math is easy to follow and the concept of compounding is clear, let's assume we have $100,000 earning 10 percent for 20 years. At the end of the year, one account would have grown by $10,000. Under the requirement of compound interest rules, what are you going to do with your interest earned? Correct! You are going to reinvest or roll it into year two. Now your account value at the beginning of the year is $110,000, but by year's end the account value has grown by $11,000. What will you do with the $11,000 of interest earned? Yes, roll it over again. Your account value at the end of year two has grown to $121,000. You are now beginning to experience the phase of interest earning interest. Take a look at the numbers below to see this play out over the first three years. In three short years you have earned $31,000 of interest.

Year	Balance Beginning Year	Annual Interest Earned	Balance End Year	Total Interest Earned
1	$100,000	$10,000	$110,000	$10,000
2	$110,000	$11,000	$121,000	$21,000
3	$121,000	$12,100	$133,100	$33,100

If you are excited about the first three years of compounding, let's look at a 20-year period to see the effects of compounding in an ideal world. As you can see below, your original investment of $100,000 grew to $672,750 by the end of year 20. Compound interest in an ideal world would literally be the eighth wonder of the world if we could actually earn 10 percent year over year without taxes, inflation or other eroding factors. Would you say compounding is good or bad at this point? I would say it's great. I think most reasonable people would agree. So what's the problem? Break out the small print.

Year	Balance Beginning Year	Annual Interest Earned	Balance End Year	Total Interest Earned
1	$100,000	$10,000	$110,000	$10,000
2	$110,000	$11,000	$121,000	$21,000
3	$121,000	$12,100	$133,100	$33,100
4	$133,100	$13,310	$146,410	$46,410
5	$146,410	$14,641	$161,051	$61,051
6	$161,051	$16,105	$177,156	$77,156
7	$177,156	$17,715	$194,872	$94,872
8	$194,872	$19,487	$214,359	$114,359
9	$214,359	$21,436	$235,795	$135,795
10	$235,795	$23,579	$259,374	$159,374
11	$259,374	$25,937	$285,312	$185,312
12	$285,312	$28,531	$313,843	$213,843
13	$313,843	$31,384	$345,227	$245,227
14	$345,227	$34,523	$379,750	$279,750
15	$379,750	$37,975	$417,725	$317,725
16	$417,725	$41,773	$459,497	$359,497
17	$459,497	$45,950	$505,447	$405,447
18	$505,447	$50,545	$555,992	$455,992
19	$555,992	$55,599	$611,591	$511,591
20	$611,591	$61,159	$672,750	$572,750

Now that you have seen compounding in an ideal world or the world that shows the large print, we have to examine the above scenarios with taxation thrown into the mix. Since we do not live in an ideal, the next logical approach is to understand how those erod-ing factors affect our wealth potential. If we go back to the 20-year compounding example above, what column did we forget to take into account? If you said taxation, pass Go on the financial game board, but don't be so quick to collect your winnings. There is more to the story than meets the eye. Knowing we did not account for taxes is a partial answer. You have to go back to define the rule of compound interest. If you compound your interest in your taxable investment account, who pays for the taxes on the growth of the account? If the bells and whistles are going off in your head, you are beginning to develop a positive money philosophy. You are the one paying the taxes, but with another source of money or out-of-pocket cost.

Let's add the additional column accounting for tax. We will assume that you are in a 25 percent marginal tax bracket and all of the interest is taxed at that ordinary income tax rate. For those of you who are ready to pounce on me for making all of the gain taxable at ordinary rates instead of blending ordinary and capital gains, please understand that I am giving the example in its simplest form for educational purposes only. Remember, this additional tax column is an additional cost that you are paying out-of-pocket if you are truly compounding your account. So let's review the facts:

1. You started with a beginning balance of $100,000 in the first year.
2. Your money compounded 10 percent annually in a taxable account.

3. Your assumed marginal tax rate equals 25 percent in all years illustrated.

4. Each year, you compounded your money, which means you chose to roll over your interest earned every year for 20 years.

5. Your cumulative interest grew to $572,750 by the end of year 20.

6. Your cumulative out-of-pocket taxes grew to $143,188 by the end of year 20.

Review the numbers on the following page. Have financial institutions taught you how to compound in a way that works in our best interest or theirs?

Compound Interest Affect with Taxation at 25%

Year	Balance Beginning Year	Annual Interest Earned	Balance End Year	Total Interest Earned	Out of Pocket Tax	Total Out Pocket Taxes Paid
1	$100,000	$10,000	$110,000	$10,000	$2,500	$2,500
2	$110,000	$11,000	$121,000	$21,000	$2,750	$5,250
3	$121,000	$12,100	$133,100	$33,100	$3,025	$8,275
4	$133,100	$13,310	$146,410	$46,410	$3,327	$11,602
5	$146,410	$14,641	$161,051	$61,051	$3,660	$15,263
6	$161,051	$16,105	$177,156	$77,156	$4,026	$19,289
7	$177,156	$17,716	$194,872	$94,872	$4,429	$23,718

8	$194,872	$19,487	$214,359	$114,359	$4,872	$28,590
9	$214,359	$21,436	$235,795	$135,795	$5,359	$33,949
10	$235,795	$23,580	$259,374	$159,374	$5,895	$39,844
11	$259,374	$25,937	$285,312	$18,5312	$6,484	$46,328
12	$285,312	$28,531	$313,843	$213,843	$7,133	$53,461
13	$313,843	$31,384	$345,227	$245,227	$7,846	$61,307
14	$345,227	$34,523	$379,750	$279,750	$8,631	$69,938
15	$379,750	$37,975	$417,725	$317,725	$9,494	$79,431
16	$417,725	$41,773	$459,497	$359,497	$10,443	$89,874
17	$459,497	$45,950	$505,447	$405,447	$11,487	$101,362
18	$505,447	$50,545	$555,992	$455,992	$12,636	$113,998
19	$555,992	$55,599	$611,591	$511,591	$13,900	$127,898
20	$611,591	$61,159	$672,750	$572,750	$15,290	$143,188

The illustrated account represents the impact taxes have when compounding your interest in a taxable account. To get $572,750 of interest in your account, you have to spend $143,188 out-of-pocket so your account can compound at a rate of 10 percent annually. When you compound a taxable account you run the risk of also compounding your tax payments. Doing so carries the cost of the tax itself and the cost of out-of-pocket tax payments lost at interest.

Simply put, you now have an opportunity cost on your out-of pocket tax payments. If we took the compounding effect of taxes over 20 years at a net rate of 7.25 percent, our tax and opportunity cost on the tax would grow to $247,965 over the twenty-year period. To get $572,750 in our account earning 10 percent, we have to spend an additional $247,965 in taxes and opportunity cost.

So you should be asking yourself, "What do I do to create a money philosophy and wealth-purposed plan that reduces the eroding factors of compounding?" A possible solution is to flatten the interest earned by moving it to a more tax favored account. By doing so, you will significantly reduce your taxes and the opportunity cost of compounding those taxes at interest. The key principles here would be to:

1. Utilize your money the way banks do. Keep it moving instead of performing only one duty, like compounding on itself.
2. Seek to pick up multiple benefits and money supply by keeping your dollars in motion.
3. Set a goal to pay a flat tax on earnings by not allowing the account to compound on itself.
4. Look for financial products or instruments that are tax-free, so you can move your interest earned from taxable accounts to accounts that are more tax favored. Also, consider using products that give you multiple benefits and protection beyond the return on investment. More on this in Chapter 10.
5. Join The Black Box Society™ where you can research, learn and experience financial strategies that will help you maximize benefits and money supply by reducing your

compounded tax effect associated with traditional compounding strategies taught by financial institutions.

"Opportunity is missed by most people because it is dressed in overalls and looks like work" - Thomas Edison

8

Who in the Middle Class Can Afford College Anyway?

"I don't believe we are supposed to go through life defeated and not having enough money to pay our bills or send our kids to college." - Joel Osteen

If you are like me, you wish nothing but the best for your children and you want to give them the best education possible. Unfortunately, the increasing cost of college is putting that dream out of reach for so many middle-class families. The national average for college tuition is more than doubling the rate of inflation on an annual basis. Without a positive money philosophy and a well designed wealth-purposed plan, most middle-class families will not be able to keep pace with the skyrocketing cost of a college education. Many families will have to sacrifice other financial wants to make up the shortfall.

According to the College Board, tuition expenses are increasing by nearly 5 percent annually at private schools and 8 percent annually at state schools. When you add up the expenses -

tuition, room and board, transportation, books and the calls home asking for extra spending money - you can expect to spend over $21,000 a year at a state school and as much as $42,000 a year at a private university. There is a second issue to consider; most kids in state schools rarely finish their undergrad in four years.

According to the U.S. Department of Education, less than 40 percent of students who enter college will graduate in four years, though most undergraduate degree programs are designed around that time frame. The study went on to say that almost 60 percent of students in an undergrad program graduate in six years. The stats are even worse for state schools where less than 33 percent of students graduate on time. This translates to more expenses, the potential for additional debt and less money in retirement for parents. The students also suffer because they miss out on two years in the workforce or pursuing entrepreneurial endeavors.

With rising costs and extended stays, a family with two children in college for a total of six or eight years could spend as much as $350,000 on higher education. That is a third more than what most couples spend on their first home and ironically, you get 30 years to finance a home. The future impact and opportunity cost of inefficient college planning could potentially have an $800,000 impact on your retirement if you use the example above. If you have more than two children in college, the numbers could easily tip the million dollar mark.

"If a man empties his purse into his head, no one can take it from him. An investment in knowledge always pays the highest return." - Ben Franklin

I really am an eternal optimist and I do believe there is hope for funding your child's education; however, I do have a keen sense of reality. I know that most middle-class parents look at their child's education cost as a single financial event, abandoning the thought that it should be part of their overall macroeconomic wealth plan. Your silver lining could be learning to develop a positive money philosophy that includes education cost as part of your overall wealth-purposed plan. Your chance at financial success will increase and the risk of impacting retirement will decrease if you react to the financial event with a positive money philosophy and wealth-purposed plan that approaches each future financial event from a micro and macro financial viewpoint.

As you have learned in previous chapters, the only successful way to manage the black box secrets for college planning is through proper use of wealth strategies. When designing a wealth-purposed plan you must take into account the true cost of education and how to efficiently and effectively pay for that education. It is important to dispel some common adopted money philosophies about how education will be funded. Many parents have adopted the belief that they earn too much to get any financial aid. Your income is only one of seven major factors used to determine your federal financial aid eligibility. I have also heard parents say they cannot afford to send their child to a private university because it is so much more expensive than a state school. This may be true at face value, but most private schools have more financial aid programs available for you to choose from and offer work-study programs that are managed around the student's school schedule.

Private schools also have a great track record of students graduating on time. This could translate to less out-of-pocket cost even if the tuition is slightly higher. Many parents also believe their debt load is a factor in determining financial aid. In reality, your debt will have no bearing on your Expected Family Contribution unless you have defaulted on a federally subsidized loan. If so, you may not get any assistance from federal school loan programs. Computing the amount of federal aid you will be eligible for is based on seven basic factors. This is not an exhausted list for computing aid, but simply the common factors used to compute your eligibility.

Basic Factors for Federal Financial Aid Eligibility

1. The amount of income earned by the parents and child.
2. The size of your family.
3. The number of children enrolled in college.
4. The amount of assets owned by the parents and student.
5. The age of the oldest parent.

6. The cost of the college you plan to attend.

7. The following also impacts eligibility: Citizenship, selective service, the chosen degree program, any default on a federal education loan, high school diploma or GED, and a drug possession or illicit drug sales conviction in your recent past.

It is imperative to complete your FAFSA each year as close to January 1 as possible. The schools you apply to will use the results to build an award package for the fall semester of that calendar year, as well as the spring and summer semesters in the next calendar year. Your award will vary from school to school in size and types of aid offered. The type of aid you can receive breaks down into federal and state sponsored grants, and work-study programs funded by your school. The federal government alone awarded more than $125 billion dollars in financial aid in 2012. If you want a share of that money, you have to decide it is worth the time to complete the *Free Application for Federal Student Aid,* know as a FAFSA form. Research and negotiate your options with the school's financial aid office and execute your college funding plan as it relates to your overall wealth-purposed plan.

When it comes to saving for college, it is important to know there are many prepackaged, traditional products that can help. There are also non-traditional instruments that can be used to fund your plan. Each plan will have its own specific advantages and disadvantages to consider. Your choices in the financial marketplace usually include the 529 plan, Coverdell Education Savings Accounts, U.S.

Savings Bonds, Education IRAs, and Uniform Gifts to Minors Act accounts, home equity loans or lines marketed for school funding. The most popular plan by far is the 529 plan. Its origin can be traced back to the state of Michigan, but the 529 plan that exists today was designed by federal lawmakers in 1996. It was named after section 529 of Internal Revenue Code 26 U.S.C. and it has two options:

- A prepaid tuition plan that allows parents, grandparents or other individuals to prepay a child's future tuition and fees at today's rates.
- A college savings plan that allows parents, grandparents and other individuals to pay into, in some cases on a pre-tax basis, an account for the student's qualified higher education expenses at an eligible higher learning institution.

Today, prepaid tuition plans are currently offered by 17 states, and 49 states and the District of Columbia offer college savings plans. Private universities and colleges are getting in the game as well. A group of 300 plus schools offer what they have termed the Independent 529 Plan. This plan allows contributors to purchase discounted tuition from any of the schools that participate in the program.

On the surface college funding with a 529 Plan seems like a very reasonable and prudent way to pay for your student's education. However, like the issues we discussed in Chapter 5 regarding qualified retirement plans, you should exercise caution in how you use a qualified education product to solve the single financial need of funding your child's education. These tax advantaged plans are designed to solve only one problem at time. That means your money can only be used to pay for education, thereby losing the opportunity to use your money for other needs that arise during your financial journey. Remember, your wealth-purposed plan should be focused on a process not a product solution approach. If you lock up your money for the single goal of giving your child an education, you could be costing yourself thousands of dollars in lost opportunity cost.

Maybe you're asking yourself, "How could I pay for the cost of my child's education and then recoup all of my money?" Better yet, "How could I guarantee my child's education through market declines, interest rate volatility, disabilities or death? What if I get sued or costs skyrocket?" If you are asking yourself theses questions then you are beginning to develop your money philosophy by simply asking, "How can I?" "How could I?" And, "What if I?" You will only begin to find a wealth-purposed solution by asking yourself the questions that you currently have no answer or solution for.

Most middle-class Americans have been taught to identify a financial goal, then figure out its shortfall and put enough money away to reach that goal. Needs-based planning usually ends up being the most expensive and least efficient way to pay for education or anything else. In the case of needs-based planning for school, the money that you will pay a college or university will be lost forever. You will never be able to use that money again. Once your child enters school and starts using the money, you have no future liquidity, use or control over that money. It is gone.

Ask yourself this: "What if my child decides they do not want to go to college?" With typical tax advantaged plans, like a 529, your tax deferral is gone and you pay income taxes at ordinary rates. You are also subject to a 10 percent penalty. "So what's the solution," you ask. Here are four things you can start doing now:

Four Steps to a Wealth-Purposed Education Plan

1. Start planning for your child's education now. Stop procrastinating.
2. Avoid prepackaged products for college funding or needs-based planning.
3. Avoid keeping all your money for college in one specific financial product.
4. Start today by designing your positive money philosophy and wealth-purposed plan. Enroll in the *KP&CO 90-Day Wealth Mastery Course™*.

"We came to Kenny with a need for money to pay for college for my step-daughter. He not only helped us find the money (within our own assets) to cover the first several years, but taught me how to negotiate with the final two college choices, resulting in both schools offering discounts or "scholarships" bringing the price within our budget. From there, we began planning and then implementing specific actions that make sense. The credit goes to Kenny and his

team for making my husband and I see the light about actively planning for our future, not just dreaming about it!"
- Judy Hamann

When designing your education funding goal within the context of your overall wealth-purposed plan, look for strategies and processes that will take into account the following:

- True tax deferral without relinquishing control to the financial institution.
- Find out how much financial aid you can get.
- Look for protection from the eroding factors that could destroy your college plan such as premature death, disabilities, law suits, market losses, income tax and penalties, opportunity cost and planned obsolescence of government education plans.
- Tax-free access to your money under any circumstance.
- Liquidity, use and control over your money.
- Enroll risk-free in the *KP&CO 90-Day Wealth Mastery Course*™

"Education costs money, but then so does ignorance."
– Sir Claus Moser

9

Life Insurance; What Is in It for Me?

"There are worse things in life than death. Have you ever spent an evening with an insurance salesman?" – Woody Allen

Life insurance ranks at the top of most everyone's list as a financial product they probably should buy, but because it evokes more mixed emotions than almost any other financial purchase it gets passed up for something more enjoyable. In the mind of most consumers it is just another bill to add to the pile. For most it is hard to quantify the value of life insurance until something bad happens or a family member dies. Unfortunately, when death knocks on your door it will be too late for you to measure its importance in your life, the life of your family and society at large.

The monetary value of your life can be measured economically. My goal in this chapter is to expose you to the black box secrets of buying and owning life insurance. I will discuss the benefits on a personal economic level and teach you how to develop a positive money philosophy and wealth-purposed plan that includes a life insurance policy, one that will be a benefit while you are living and a blessing to those you love when you die.

Let's focus first on why you would buy life insurance. I personally believe that every person eligible should own life insurance. We all have an economic value and anything of value should be insured against possible loss. The lifetime value of one's ability to earn and produce income should be protected. Most life insurance companies have a policy regarding how much you can own. The maximum amount is based predominantly on the value of your economic life. In most cases, an insurance company will give you up to twenty-five times your income or the one-time net value of your estate.

Unfortunately, many consumers will never hear this message because the overwhelming majority of insurance salespeople have been trained in the needs analysis selling process. Under this selling strategy, consumers get less than what they could have had if given the opportunity to purchase the maximum death benefit. The focus shifts from the insured to the beneficiary when using a needs approach to selling life insurance. If you were to ask anyone facing cancer or a deadly disease what they would want to leave their family, the answer would be the maximum possible benefit. The problem is most of us only think in those terms when we are faced with an event that could be life altering.

Think of it in terms that are easier to discuss. I am not trying to push you into a casket. Let's say you came home one day to find your house had burned to the ground. What is the first question you would ask your insurance agent? My guess is you would be asking them about the replacement value of your home. Why? Because you simply want your house back not a FEMA-issued double-wide trailer. If you owned your homeowners insurance the way most of us own life insurance you would have to settle for the trailer, which is good news if you hate your neighbors. Now you can wheel your home to another location. But in all seriousness, what reason would anyone have to not buy the best insurance possible if they knew their house was going to burn down tomorrow? The same goes for life insurance. If you were going to die tomorrow, you would want the best policy possible.

OK, I'm guessing you have one logical reason not to own the maximum policy - cost. Your reason is valid not only for life insurance, but for car insurance and homeowners insurance, as well as liability, disability, and major medical insurance. What if you could employ a positive money philosophy and wealth-purposed plan that allowed for the maximum benefits with little to no additional outlay of capital from your current plan? Or in other words, if life insurance were free, how much would you own? All you could get, right? It is feasible to do if you decide, commit and execute a wealth-purposed plan that seeks to maximize protection benefits while simultaneously improving money flow and inefficiencies in your current plan.

When I work with new clients and we get to this point in the wealth mastery process, they are often a little skeptical about how this can be accomplished. After they have learned to look at their wealth-plan using their own positive money philosophy, it becomes very clear how to proceed in purchasing protection products and making a decision regarding life insurance.

Life insurance is designed to do many things for the owner. Insurance companies spend millions of dollars each year telling us to buy their products. The most popular way that life insurance is marketed is death protection. Death protection is typically marketed and solved with the use of term insurance. Term insurance is a great tool to maximize your overall death benefit for short-term periods. It usually costs the least to fund upfront, but can easily become the most expensive to you and your estate in the long run. Many financial gurus pontificate on buying pure death benefits using term insurance only.

As such with most financial products, consumers take the gurus' advice and apply the adopted principles without completely verifying whether or not it is the best option for their own plan. This mistake typically costs consumers millions of dollars in lost opportunity cost at their own expense and the expense of their family. The gurus forgot to tell you about the odds. Statistics vary insurance company to insurance company, but most will admit that less than 5 percent of their term policies ever payout as a death claim. Some companies have even reported term death claims at less than 0.25 percent. So 99.75 percent of the premiums they take in become gross profit. Think about that stat in terms of gambling.

If you could fly to Las Vegas and be 99.75 percent sure you could win one hand of black jack, how much money would you bet on that one hand? The answer: as much as reasonably possible without bankrupting yourself if by chance you lose the hand. That's what the insurance company does with every consumer that buys term life insurance. They, however, do not have to put their money down on just one hand. They get to see multiple hands over and over again. Every so often they lose a few, but the odds are overwhelmingly in their favor.

As you have learned in previous chapters, every decision you make has its own advantages and disadvantages, as well as potential for high returns and risk of loss. You have to account for the opportunity cost associated with your financial decisions. I am not saying term insurance is a bad product. I am simply asking you to consider the entire objective before deciding on your method. If you believe you will live to the average age of 78.64 years, then you should consider owning the life insurance policy that provides living benefits to you as well as a death benefit to your heirs. If you become a member of The Black Box Society™, you will learn verifiable strategies for how to own your life insurance throughout your life and leave a legacy to those you love.

There are numerous merits and flaws in all types of life insurance products in the marketplace today. My belief system tells me to keep it basic and to go with what has been in the marketplace the longest. When we are talking life insurance that product is whole life insurance. I know some of you are now closing the book or powering down your device. But before you walk away, please remember you hold the power to make the best decision possible for your wealth-purposed plan. You also hold the power to develop your own positive money philosophy. So if you do not agree with me, that's OK as long as you are keeping an open mind and truly discovering what strategies work best in your own plan. I just ask that you verify what you believe to be true by examining and challenging your previous truths within the confines of new knowledge.

From my experiences, people avoid whole life insurance for two reasons – they think it is too expensive and they do not see a need for future life insurance coverage. Earlier in the chapter, I asked you how much life insurance you would own if it were free. My question now is how much whole life insurance would you own if it were free? Before you answer let's examine the basics.

Insurance companies understand their risk better than anyone. So why would they charge a 40-year-old male $700 a year for a million dollars in death benefit protection? This particular term contract has a level death benefit and level premium for 20 years. On the other hand, they now insure another 40-year-old male in the same rating class and charge him $16,300 a year for the same million-dollar death benefit. The reason is actuarial risk. The insurance company knows that only 5 percent of policyholders will die during the level term period. The contracts for the other 95 percent expired in year 20. Those who made it not only lost their premium at interest, they lost their million-dollar death benefit. Those costs add up to over $2.5 million dollars in lost premiums and death benefit at interest for the consumer. The insurance company keeps this premium as low as possible so they can attract as many healthy customers as possible. If the field force sells the most profitable product and listens to its actuaries, the insurance company will win virtually every time.

On the other hand, insurance companies have other policyholders who are still living and quite healthy. If that policyholder bought participating, dividend-paying, whole life insurance, that policy by year 20 will have grown to $1.5 million in death benefits with a cash value account over $550,000. The insurance company has to assume that this policyholder will keep his policy until his or her death. If the policyholder in this example died at 79, the insurance company would have to contractually pay a death benefit of $2.6 million dollars, income tax free, to the beneficiary. That's the equivalent of a taxable account earning about 10 percent on the premium deposits over 39 years.

During the premium paying years, the insurance company also has to account for the policyholder being able to have liquidity, use and control over his premium payments and dividends. In this case, the policyholder had access to most of his cash during his accumulation years, growing it to over $1.5 million in cash value by age 79 to use in the family's wealth-purposed plan. The insurance company also had to factor in the risk of this person becoming disabled during the premium payment years until age 65. If disability had occurred, the insurance company would continue to pay the premiums on the insured's behalf and the policy would stay in place, allowing the cash value to grow at the same rate it would have if the insured was paying the premium. The premium payments not only purchased death benefits, they also accumulated cash value along with the possibility of earning a dividend.

Although the dividend is not guaranteed, almost all mutually held insurance companies have a history of paying dividends, in some cases for over 100 years. Unlike dividends in your stock accounts, once a dividend is paid to a policyholder it can never be taken back or lost if the market declines. The policyholder's beneficiary also enjoys tax deferred growth and access to the cash income tax-free, as long as the policy stayed in force or paid out as a death benefit. While this policyholder was living, the insurance company had to account for all of the above variables. Then, upon the policyholder's death, they contractually had to pay the policyholder's beneficiary the entire death benefit income tax-free.

Hopefully, you now have a better understanding of what is in it for you when considering life insurance. Regardless of your slant toward term insurance or permanent life insurance, you should consider owning the maximum amount that the insurance company will issue you. Once you know the maximum amount, you can decide how much you want on your own instead of listening to some guru tell you how much you need. You can then decide how much you want to deposit and save on an annual basis in your whole life insurance contract. In most cases, a properly trained wealth coach can find inefficiencies in your current plan and help you find a way to pay for life insurance without spending new money. Here are some tips to consider when deciding how to include life insurance in your positive money philosophy and master your wealth:

- Consult your agent about the maximum amount of life insurance you can purchase, not what he or she believes you need.
- If you do not want to contact your agent, then contact *Kenneth Porter & Company, Ltd.* and we will refer you to an agent in your area who is trained to fund life insurance properly.
- Consider the value of whole life insurance in your wealth-purposed plan and if you think you want it for your entire life.
- Examine the living benefits of whole life insurance.
- Discover the benefits and multiple uses of life insurance in a wealth-purposed plan so you can achieve true wealth mastery in your life.
- Enroll risk-free in the *KP&CO 90-Day Wealth Mastery Course*™ so you can learn and implement true wealth building strategies.

"Believe that life is worth living and your belief will help create the fact." - William James

10

How Do I Maximize My Wealth Mastered Plan?

"The farmer has to be an optimist or he wouldn't still be a farmer." - Will Rogers

Sometimes having unbridled access to more and more information can cause additional confusion when deciding what's best for your life and money. We often take for granted the ability to educate ourselves with the click of a button and we procrastinate so much so that we never truly maximize our best life or money purpose.

It is up to each of us to take full responsibility for maximizing our greatest wealth potential in our lifetime. The education, tools and products are available for you to use in your own wealth-purposed plan, but the responsibility simply lies in your own hands. Only you can fulfill you financial destiny.

If people decided, committed and executed every well-meaning financial goal that they set, I believe we would see more people in the world mastering their wealth. Unfortunately, our society is saving money at an all time low, consumers are accumulating more debt and bankruptcies are still on the rise. If you decide today that your money philosophy needs to improve, then you will need to take action and commit to change. Once you have committed to financial change, stick with it and execute your wealth-purposed goals until you have reached your financial destination.

Do not fall prey to get-rich-quick schemes that often plague our financial marketplace. Ask yourself, "Is it too good to be true?" Remember the wise words of President Ronald Reagan, "Trust, but verify." Everyone would love to be wealthy, but truly verifying how possible it is through your own wealth-mastered plan will save you countless disappointments and thousands of dollars in lost cost. The foundation for developing and then maximizing your wealth-mastered plan is cemented in developing a positive money philosophy. Your wealth should be built on a solid foundation of savings and sound investments, not some get-rich-quick scheme.

Learning how to properly protect, build and grow your wealth will not protect you from failure. Every so often a financial event may occur that sets you back and disrupts your wealth plan. The greatest disruptions, however, typically happen within the mind. We simply allow the financial event to trigger limited money beliefs, which keep us from achieving our wealth goals. The key to removing the limited belief when failure occurs is to change your response. When you respond with a positive money belief, you will see change occur in the money result. The only guarantee we have in life is death. Knowing life ends should push us to become purposeful and live the best financial life possible. Time cannot be reversed. Start your journey and find *The Billionaire Within*™.

Think of your positive money philosophy as the guide to finding *The Billionaire Within*™. It is impossible to predict the future, but it is possible to lay a course for the future. If you look back on the last year of your life, you can clearly see how you arrived at your current destination. God has blessed you with talents, resources and a desire to seek out a better financial life than the one you are currently living. He cannot fulfill the desires in your heart unless you become a willing instrument that is submissive and open to the possibilities of what can be achieved. May God bless you many times over. Remember to believe in the possibility of a billionaire within.

Maximize Your Wealth Mastered Plan

- Make small changes to improve your current plan.
- Commit to developing and sharpening your wealth plan so that wealth mastery can be achieved.
- Execute your positive money philosophy and become committed to living a wealth-purposed life.
- Join The Black Box Society™.

"You must be the change you wish to see in the world."
- Mahatma Gandhi

Resources / Information / Financial Education

- Imagine the possibilities of what you could accomplish with your own wealth coach. Enroll for *FREE* Wealth Coaching at: **www.kennethporterandco.com**

- Discover how to maximize your wealth potential by enrolling in the: *KP&CO 90-Day Wealth Mastery Course*™ **www.kennethporterandco.com/wealth-coaching/ 90-days-to-wealth-mastery**

- Read more about: **"Our Big Goal"** **www.kennethporterandco.com/about-kenneth-porter/the-275-foundation**

- Learn how to join: **The Black Box Society**™ **www.theblackboxsociety.net**

- Share the experience of the book with others: **The Billionaire Within**™ **www.thebillionairewithin.net**

9 780989 380218